FOOTBALLS BIGGEST EVER JOKE BOOK

by

Gary Rowley

They say it's a funny old game – well, it is now, anyway!

This fabulously funny football joke book is a must have companion for all devotees of the beautiful game. With over 1000 mostly original gags, it's guaranteed to have you in stitches and choking on your half time cup of Bovril. Good, clean fun, it would be equally at home in the hands of kids or grandparents, while still providing ample ammunition to consign your mates down the pub to an early bath.

All you need to do to become immersed in this maelstrom of madcap mayhem is find a quiet corner somewhere then slowly turn the page...

Enjoy!

For all my friends at Billy Clarke's fishing tackle shop in Sheffield – even if they are Blades!

FRINGE PLAYER

I spotted Rio Ferdinand on his way home from the big game with a mannequin under his arm. I thought, whey hey, someone's sold him a dummy.

The letterbox rattled and this eight foot length of six-by-four landed with a resounding thump on the carpet. I shouted, the post has arrived, darling.

Did you hear about the footballer who couldn't stop burping? It was a freak hic'.

All this criticism of Rafa Benitez for playing a flat back four is bang out of order if you ask me. What else was he expected to do when his defence had just been run over by a steamroller?

What did the manager of the Potato Growers' Association football team say during the half time team talk? It's all about Desiree...

Sportsflash: Animal rights activists are camped outside Manchester United's training ground after it was announced Wayne Rooney has injured a calf.

I've just turned down a dream move to Paris Saint Germain. I must have been in Seine.

What do you get if you cross a former Sheffield United and England footballer with the country's longest running soap? Tony Corrie.

I've just seen the American football scores. Hawaii won five-0.

A Premiership footballer called the press complaints commission when his new IPhone started leaking water? A spokesman confirmed it had been tapped.

Humpty Dumpty's stint at football management didn't last very long: he cracked under the pressure.

I was filling in this application form and had to provide the names of two referees. I eventually plumped for Howard Webb and Pierre Luigi Collina.

A constipated Sam Allardyce went to the chemists, and the same girl was in again, the one who used to work at McDonalds. He said, can I have a box of laxatives, please? She said, to go? He said, what do you think?

Did you hear about the chain-smoking manager, the one whose team were bottom of the league? Fans clubbed together to buy him a cigarette lighter because he was always losing matches.

I saw this big, pink footballer, with yellow spots, and strands of hair combed carefully across his scalp. It was Blobby Charlton.

The truckers' footy team have made a great start to the season. But it won't last: it's only a matter of time before the wheels come off...

When Chelsea's new manager emerged from the tunnel, wearing blue overalls, and carrying a mop and bucket, it quickly became apparent that Roman Abramovich had appointed another caretaker.

I spent a fortune following Dundee United's pre-season tour of Venezuela: I must have been Caracas!

No wonder Fergie has enjoyed such fantastic success. In the pre-match interview, he predicted Messi would be utilised in a holding roll. Lo and behold, come kick off, there was Messi, holding a cheese and salad sandwich...

This bloke was adamant all the world's great ships had docked in Liverpool. I disagreed. I said, what about The Premiership?

Football: it's just not cricket.

I've just seen a bus in a tracksuit outside Elland Road. It must have been one of the coaches.

Portsmouth supporter's club aren't too concerned about the team's meteoric fall from grace. Someone has assured them there are 20,000 leagues under the sea.

We lost 1-0 to Battersea Dogs Home. Jack Russell got the winner.

Arsene Wenger ensured Arsenal's losing streak continued when he ran naked through the streets of Islington after a 1-0 home defeat to French side Newcastle United.

I was en route to watch Barnsley play Sheffield Wednesday when this dee-dar flagged me down and offered me a tenner to help him get his broken down car going. I told him where to shove it.

With the big match a white-out, Rooney left the car behind and set off walking home. Just past Wilmslow, he had a near miss with a hurtling snow plough. Watch where you're going! he screamed, through gritted teeth...

Victoria Beckham was reported to be disappointed with the new chick flick Premiere she attended with David. It was all about a hen, playing Subbuteo.

David persuaded her to go with him to see the new A-Team movie the day after, but she didn't like that, either. She thought it was all about Face.

I was invited to a fancy dress party and there was this bloke with a football pools coupon, pinned to his torso. Apparently he'd come as a chest of draws.

People mock when I tell them I used to be Gillingham's head groundsman. I don't know why. I'll have you know I was outstanding in my field.

Rumour has it the manager of the TV aerial company football team resigned just before midnight. No doubt we'll get a better picture in the morning.

I couldn't believe it when I saw Chesterfield were top of the league. Then I realised: I was holding my newspaper upside down!

We played a friendly against this team from the Monopoly, Cluedo & Ludo Plastic Dice Manufacturing Company. It should have been no contest, but they were better than we thought: for a good half hour, they didn't half have us at sixes and sevens...

Spiderman is really a Premiership referee. The clue's in the name: it's Howard Webb.

I went to watch Northampton Town play: what a load of cobblers.

Two Argentinian footballers had a dust up. It was Juan on Juan.

I was on holiday in Africa with Paul Ince. He kicked this Tarantula, and the Tarantula went, ouch! It was an Incey wincing spider.

Torres scored his first goal in three months then punched the air. Abramovich threw his son a steak for the black eye then loaned the Spaniard out to Bradford City until 2020.

Did you see that documentary last night about the shipbuilder's football team? It was absolutely riveting.

What a brilliant match: it was slim, two inches long, and had a pink, phosphorous head.

I was in this pub in Portsmouth, watching Tranmere Rovers take on Shrewsbury Town through the window. I couldn't believe it: the bloke on the next table actually thought it was on the tele!

Alex Ferguson's kitchen ceiling has been ruled out of Saturday's big game: it's suspended.

I've lost my plaice in the fishmonger's select XI: I'm absolutely gutted.

Under pressure over spiralling electricity costs, MK Dons' head groundsman was caught smearing strawberry jam over the club's electrical points. He explained he was conserving energy.

The new manager of the pet shop footy team, it's Kenny Dogleash.

I'm struggling to get the Best out of my son. How he managed to swallow a bronze statuette of Man United's famous Irish winger is completely beyond me.

Middlesbrough entertained Watford: they organised a comedian and puppet show then finished off with a nice finger buffet.

It's the Herb Association challenge cup final tonight. I bet it goes to extra thyme.

There was this football agent, walking into Anfield with Samir Nasri on his head. I think he was doing a balance transfer.

I found this almanac, containing all next season's football results. Talk about a know-win situation.

Did you hear about the Scouse street artist, who celebrated Everton's win in the Merseyside derby by painting the town blue?

Harry Redknapp blasted the edge of the six yard box with a shotgun then sold it to Spurs: it was transfer dead line day.

I went on an away day to Hertha Berlin and fell out with everyone I met. I must have been having a bad Herr day.

After ten defeats in a row for the meteorologists' football team, I fear my rain as manager may finally be over...

If you receive junk mail, claiming to contain free tickets to watch Sheffield United, do not, under any circumstances, consider opening it: it contains free tickets to watch Sheffield United.

Manchester City took to the field in filthy shirts and mud-stained shorts: Mancini had named an unchanged side.

Apparently Posh Spice lost the diamond out of her ring during Sunday dinner. Now she sticks her head down the pot every time she goes to the toilet, convinced it will turn up eventually. David's not so sure, mind: he thinks she's just going through the motions.

I phoned Torquay United. I said, what time is kick off? This voice said, what time can you get here...?

Kevin Keegan has finally landed a job with no pressure. He mends broken water mains.

The first team squad arrived at the ground with their jackets on fire. I thought, whey hey, club blazers!

I went to the footy and all the players were engrossed in this word game in the penalty area. It was a goalmouth Scrabble.

My new milk round in Anfield: it doesn't half take some Bootle.

The match was goalless. So Owen and Jagielka threw a couple of coats down.

We drew Goole Town in the cup on Halloween. The goalkeeper was a zombie and the centre forward a free-floating, full-torso, vaporous apparition. A poltergeist scored the winner with a real screamer...

I've just signed a pre-contract agreement with Kathmandu United: they're convinced I can do a job at that level.

Berbatov placed the ball in the quadrant then lit a fag: it was smoker's corner.

South East Asia's footballer of the year recently moved from Pyongyang United to Seoul City. He needed a change of Korea.

So I said to Howard Webb, that thingamajig round your wrist that tells the time: watchamacallit?

I suspect the new GP down the surgery leads a double life as a football hooligan. He has a skinhead haircut, wears boots and braces, and everyone refers to him as Doc Martin.

The match was such a non-event, the entire crowd fell asleep, bringing a whole new meaning to the phrase, hoof it into Row Zzzz.

Sportsflash: Bristol City's Ashton Gate stadium is currently under a foot of water. Club officials are blaming a problem with the floodlights.

I once attended a football match on the moon, but can't say I enjoyed it. There was no atmosphere.

Tony Adams has been caught drinking and driving. He was swigging diet coke, whilst belting a ball two hundred yards down the fairway...

Before I turned football hooligan, I used to be a mod. I must have been off my rocker.

Did you hear about the footballer who thumped a vintage sixties coin? He turned on a sixpence.

This bloke stopped me and asked if I knew what time Notts County kicked off. I said, usually every ten minutes.

I was desperate for the toilet on a trip to London's Loftus Road. Talk about Queue, Pee, Aaah!

When Van Persie missed a penalty, I ran on the pitch, broke his legs and pushed the goalposts over. Mum packed me straight off to bed and put my Subbuteo back in the cupboard.

The fish and chip shop XI, we absolutely battered them...

Camberwick Green Rovers have offered a trial to Windy Miller. But he'll never make the grade.

I went to the game and there was the spitting image of Bruce Springsteen, sitting in the dugout. I said, is that The Boss?

Manchester City spent six million pounds on an old bloke in the park...and then left him on the bench.

Fingerless goalkeeping gloves: I can't see the point in them.

Who is the Premier League's dirtiest ever player? It's Robbie Fouler!

I offered a Spurs player called Kyle a lift to the training ground. He said, no thanks, I'm a Walker.

There was this spud, swearing its head off in the press box: it was a common-tator.

It's just been on talkSport that an eighty-eight year old German footballer scored three goals, during an incredible fifteen minute spell for Hamburg old folks' home. It was a geriatric Jerry hat-trick.

I went to Liverpool and couldn't believe how many people were on their way to see some woman called Ann Field.

The wife says all I do is lounge around, watching football, and if our marriage is to survive the weekend, we need to make time to talk. I thought, yeah, right: like that's going to happen when I've just settled down to enjoy extended highlights of Rotherham United versus Bury in the second round of the Johnstone's Paint Trophy.

I'm Yeovil Town's new first team coach. I'm racked out with seats and ferry the team to all its away matches.

When McDonald went down, clutching his neck, the trainer ran on and shouted, quick, support his head. And the crowd began to chant, McDonald's head, clap-clap-clap, McDonald's head, clap-clap-clap...

I put Sky Sports on and Gary Neville was eating tomato, Jamie Redknapp minestrone, and Martin Tyler leek and potato. It was Souper Sunday.

So the barbers' shop association are running away with Sunday league division three: so what? Mark my words: they'll come a cropper sooner or later.

There was this sign on the motorway, which said, Barnsley 9 Sheffield 26. I thought, blimey, that must have been some game!

I collect signs from round the edge of football pitches. I'm big into advertising hoarding.

Jolean Lescott walked into Burger King and asked for two whoppers. The assistant said, OK, you're a real handsome dude and Manchester City will absolutely walk the Champions League...

TIP ROUND THE POST

What's the coldest football ground in Britain? It's Brrrmingham City.

Or is it Cold Trafford?

Or the Shiverside?

Or how about Chillsborough?

Thirty-six new born cows lined up across the middle of the pitch. It was the calf way line.

I prickled my finger on a footballer: it was Titus Bramble.

Alan Pardew has been forced to withdraw a bid for Chelsea's England international full-back, the one formerly married to Cheryl Tweedy. Apparently Chairman Mike Ashley couldn't see the point taking Cole to Newcastle.

There was this ginger-haired bloke, acting really weird in the pub last night. He said his name was Alex and that he used to manage Motherwell, Hibs, Rangers, Scotland, Birmingham City, Villa and Forest. I'd keep an eye out for him if I were you: he was last seen on his way into the Jobcentre, wearing a Mac and holding a leash...

I walked in the dressing room and cats were everywhere. I said, alright, who emptied the kit bag?

Flagging linesmen: they need to get back in the gym.

What would you get if you crossed a West Midlands football team with a tub of ice-cream? Aston Vanilla!

Two down with fifteen minutes to go, City sent the sub on. I thought, right, let's see how United cope with an Astute-class, nuclear powered hunter-killer.

I've been invited to a drugs party and told I have to fetch my own dope. I wonder what David Beckham's doing on Saturday week?

The groundsman put a sign out saying, keep off the grass. Next thing, there was lots of coughing and spluttering, and red-faced supporters, hurriedly stamping out roll-ups.

I've visited football grounds all over the country, but never fancied Man City. I can't imagine what it must be like, living in a town where there aren't any women.

When the new signing from Limerick developed a migraine, the club doctor told him to go away and take a couple of tablets. A few hours later, he was back again, complaining of indigestion this time. The doctor asked what he'd eaten. He said, only what you told me: an IPad then a Kindle Fire...

The gaffer assembled our entire first team squad for only four pound coins and two fifty pence pieces. By coincidence, his favourite training ground routine is fiver-side.

I watched Leyton Orient versus Milton Keynes Dons through the window of an in-flight Boeing 707. It was on Sky Sports.

So I said, there's only one thing stopping me playing centre half for Manchester United and England. He said, what's that? I said, I'm not good enough.

Q: What do you call a world class Liverpool player? A: Retired.

I visited this football ground where all the supporters were follically challenged. It was Bald Trafford.

Did you hear about the ghost's football match? It was a late kick off.

I play Sunday league football for the umbrella factory: we're the raining champions.

I've always had a burning ambition to build a secret hideaway in the back of the net: it's my goal den goal.

I couldn't believe it when I heard Wolves had appointed some ex-university wallah as their new manager. Who is this Dean Saunders, anyway?

England to beat Brazil? You must be nuts!

Apparently Real Mallorca's Scottish international defender put the wrong shirt on and trotted out wearing the name of that Jaap bloke, the one who used to play centre half for Man United. Talk about Hutton dressed as Stam.

What did one footballer say to the other footballer? I'll meet you at the corner.

I went on this away day, where the home fans couldn't decide whether they were going to buy a Ka, Mondeo or Focus. All they sang for the full ninety minutes was, what Ford, clap-clap-clap, what Ford, clap-clap-clap, what Ford, clap-clap-clap...

Sportsflash: Newcastle's Jack and the Beanstalk Christmas Pantomime has suffered a last minute cancellation because the giant could only find Frenchmen to smell.

This bloke in the crowd said, who's that brilliant little player with five stars embroidered on each shoulder and a rake of medals pinned to his chest? I said, do you mean the midfield general?

I went to this football ground, where the pies were made from rancid meat, and the supporters were running round like Mo Farah. It was Old Ham Athletic.

My friend is football crazy. He even bought a house on Huddersfield Road in tribute to his favourite team. Just in case you wondered, I live at 64 Spearmint Rhino Avenue.

Brendan Rodgers sent a youth team player to the shop for a box of teabags, but he came back empty handed after they refused to serve him. The parched manager said it was the first he'd heard that the PG in Tips stood for parental guidance.

On a visit to United's training ground, I saw this bloke in a white coat, bandaging up a broken 4-iron. Someone said it was the club doctor.

I was on the eighteenth hole when this car went flying over my head and demolished the club house. Turned out it was Alan Hansen, having a game of VW Golf.

What would you get if you crossed a former Wales and Manchester United centre forward with a German car and a female sheep? Merc Ewes!

I asked an American soccer player if he had a favourite brand of German motor car. He said, howdy.

There's a rumour going round that Roman Abramovich is thinking of buying a new Villa. Apparently it's located in the Aston area of Birmingham.

Against all the odds, we beat Leicester away: we completely out-foxed them.

I went on a tour of White Hart Lane. As we passed the manager's office, we could hear someone singing, do-re-mi-fa-so-la-ti-do. The guide explained it was AVB, going through his programme notes.

AFC Wimbledon players have been clocked doing fifty in the 30mph zone outside the ground after realising it was the only way they were ever going to get three points.

I was on my way to the ground, adrenalin pumping, filled with expectation at the prospect of three more points to bolster our late dash for promotion. But first item on the agenda was food from the burger bar. Hot dog, I said...with relish.

The boys from the mattress factory may have made a brilliant start to the season, but now they aren't half struggling for foam...

What do Jose Mourinho and Steve McClaren have in common? They're both known as the 'Special One' except for Steve McClaren.

I looked out of the window and there was this football match, taking place on the front lawn of the house opposite. It was obviously a home game.

Arsene Wenger has booked his first team squad into dog training classes in the hope that someone can show them how to hold on to a lead.

It's been on the news that an official made a pass at Joey Barton's partner during the draw for the World Cup qualifiers. The press have labelled it the grope of death...

Someone said Peter Crouch has signed for Crawley Town. Tall story if you ask me.

I hear the gaffer has signed a world class striker from Barnsley. Apparently it's some bloke with a comb-over, who goes by the name of Scargill.

Did you hear about the alcoholic footballer's new alarm clock? It goes tick-tick, tick-tick, tick-tick: it was a present from de-tocks.

Queens Park Rangers goalkeepers: they never get the Robert the Green.

Santa's forage into football management ended abruptly when Lapland United gave him the sack...

I'd hate to be the bloke leading the sing-song at Borussia Mönchengladbach. Just imagine it: give us a B, b,b, give us an O, o,o, give us an R, r,r...

The bloke I sit next to at the match is a Vietnam vet. He treats sick animals in Hanoi.

Scientists crossed a straight talking footballer with a sugar cube and twenty-six prize Friesians. The result: Frank Lump Herd.

I saw this football agent, slipping the gaffer a stopper for sealing a hole in a container. I thought, ooh look, he's giving him a bung.

The journalists' football team are pretty good...but they're still a way off being the finished article.

I went to the match wearing one glove. It was the weatherman's fault. He said it might be cold or, on the other hand, it could be sunny.

Our misfiring centre forward, bless him, he didn't half have the crowd on his back last night. He was last seen disappearing up the tunnel with angry supporters, swinging off his shoulders.

Two spectators in Jungle Book costumes were involved in a dust-up today at the KC stadium. Honestly, it was a right Hull-a-Baloo!

What do you get if you cross a Uruguayan football manager with a large water bird? Goose Poyet.

I've got a frog in my throat. I've just swallowed Patrice Evra.

Our new midfielder took to the field with a Rolls Royce Merlin V12 strapped to his back. It was just like the manager said: brilliant engine.

An Arsenal player went on Mastermind. He passed sixty-eight times...of course he didn't win anything.

Fabio Capello turned up at Specsavers late on Saturday evening. The optician apologised and said there was nothing he could do with his broken glasses until Monday... but he did offer to board them up for him.

I hear the Boston Strangler has started watching AFC Bournemouth. If you ask me, he needs to get a grip...

It was the ninetieth minute of a gentlemanly encounter when all the players suddenly started kicking bits off one another. I thought, whey hey, injury time.

The creature off that film, the one where the occupants of an Antarctica research station discover an alien in a block of ice and then fight to stay alive as it consumes them one by one, it's just signed for Spurs, but refuses to part with the ball during training. Not that AVB is concerned. When quizzed about the situation, he said, all Things must pass...

I went to watch the Farmers' Union under 16's and couldn't have been more impressed. Honestly, what a brilliant crop of players.

There was this woman in the park with a set of goalposts on her head. Someone said her name was Annette.

The Norwegian centre forward who used to play for Villa, what's his favourite pop group? It's So Solid Carew.

I manage the Merchant Navy football team: I'm at the helm.

Arsenal's nickname is the Gunners: is this because they are always gunner but never quite do?

When the footballer agreed to a divorce, his wife took everything: the house, the car, the money, even the dog. She was the one that got her way.

Who is the world's untidiest footballer? It's Lionel Messy!

I was walking across this football field when a length of white chalk on grass asked me out on a date: it must have been the forward line.

There's a rumour going round old 'bite yer legs' hasn't got a good word to say about William Sharp of Nottingham Forest. He's Billy Norm hates.

Did you hear about the footballer who bought all the beer in the supermarket? He was playing keepy-hoppy.

Liverpool's defence: it's looking a bit Agger-ed.

I asked the wife what her favourite Al-bum was. She said, I quite like his, that Shearer bloke on Match of the Day.

We've just signed Brer Rabbit. It's a Bunny old game...

My guest appearance for the dentists' footy team went down a treat when I bagged a brace.

Commentary: And let's go live to Stamford Bridge, where the Pampers team have just taken a shock lead in the cup. It's Terry Towelling who's got it...

I turned out for a team of surgeons the week after but got subbed at half time. Not that I was surprised. I knew I would struggle with their lung ball game...

Did you hear about the footballer whose palms were covered with tufts of hair? It was Rio Furred In Hand.

The boss insisted upon playing our star striker even though he was recovering from a bout of diarrhoea. He didn't score. But he did have some brilliant runs.

Why is everyone in the Middle East Blackburn Rovers crazy? I was in Amman last week and all the radio travel news presenter could talk about was Jordan Rhodes...

I have my own box at Old Trafford. I'm only little and use it to stand on every time the crowd gets to its feet.

The manager has just signed this real handsome dude from Real Madrid: it's Looker Modrić.

Luton Town supporters: they're mad as Hatters.

What do you say to a Leeds United supporter in a suit? Would the defendant please rise...?

I went to the match and was shocked to see this medium sized, burrowing mammal, wearing bovver boots and knuckle dusters. I thought, ooh look, a haard-vark.

We've just signed a keeper with eight arms and ink for blood. Not that he's made the first team yet: he's more of a squid player.

Before Leicester City moved grounds, did you know they played at a stadium named after two lifelong supporters, twin brothers, Phil and Bert Street?

The match ball: don't strike it too hard...

I really enjoyed the post-match Celebrations at Loftus Road. It was great of the club to open a tin of free chocolates even though they'd lost again...

Someone threw a pound coin on the field at Bramall Lane. Speculation is rife it could be a takeover bid.

This Milwall fan went to the doctors. The doctor said, say aah. And the Milwall fan went, Aaargh!!!

Richard Branson has put a bid in for Birmingham City. Apparently his son wants a cowboy outfit for Christmas.

I went to this match where all the supporters were eight foot tall. Talk about a big crowd.

The whip and top football team: they've won six on the spin.

Howard Webb booked Andy Carroll. He whacked him round the head with a copy of Great Expectations.

I went to a séance with the England football team. As usual, we struggled for possession.

The lads from the leaflet and pamphlet printing company, their new season has got off to a real flier...

I went to watch a football match in the Himalayas, refereed by Joe Pesquali. It was what you might term high pitched.

The girlfriend finished with me because of my obsession with football. I still can't believe it: three and a half seasons we'd been going out...

We drew a team of egg fanatics in the cup. It was Yolk City.

Name two flowers that played football for Man United: Dennis Violet and Ted MacDougall (graded grains).

The vacuum cleaner factories XI were leading 7-0 after a brilliant forty-five minute display. The question on everyone's lips was: when the second half started, would they be able to pick up where they left off?

I couldn't believe it when the opposition started taking their clothes off in the penalty area. The bloke standing next to me said it was the new away strip.

What did Sir Alf Ramsey say to the England team just before the 1966 World Cup Final? Come on now, lads, get that kit on...

Fergie doesn't half blood them young, nowadays. Alright, so the eighteen months old kid he picked last Saturday wasn't the tallest. But he couldn't half dribble.

I play Sunday League for the local pet shop side: we're Leads United.

Anti-Semitism: is it the England football team's inability to progress beyond the quarter finals of a major tournament?

The blacksmiths' XI: we absolutely hammered them.

It's just been announced that a well-known, Sussex based Championship football club have signed a lucrative sponsorship deal with a major vacuum cleaner manufacturer. From next season, they will be known as Brighton & Hoover Albion.

I applied for a full time course at college. When I got there, it was a classroom of trainee referees, blowing whistles.

Did you hear about the footballer who had a Big Mac for dinner? Apparently he was extremely partial to XXXL raincoats.

I've just discovered I can bend it like Beckham. The doctor says I've got athlete's foot.

Johann Strauss missed a penalty for the classical music footy team. No composure.

I play in the Spanish plumbers' division: it's Loo Liga.

We were having a swift half in the penalty area when the opposition nipped through to score: they caught us on the hops.

How come French side Newcastle United are allowed to name a five subs plus the entire squad of Egyptian Premier League club Nile Rangers?

The lions lost to the big cats in a bad tempered encounter, with the felines scoring the winner courtesy of a dubious, late penalty. Interviewed straight after the game, the lion's manager said they were nothing but a bunch of cheetahs...

I went to the game and was shocked to see a bunch of old ladies in boots and braces, beating the crap out of a group of visiting supporters. I thought, ooh look, football hooligrans.

The artificial implant team is in crisis after news broke of a major dressing room bust up...

SPURS FAN

My mate's wife lost a tooth, eating a bag of pork scratchings. In defence, he did say that he warned her not to rustle paper while he was watching Fleetwood versus Morecambe in the FA Cup first round replay.

The Official attendance at Old Trafford was four: Howard Webb, two linesmen and that waste of space who holds up the additional minutes board...

I visited this Scottish football ground, where the surrounding streets were laden with chocolate eggs...it was Easter Road.

In goal we have the Royal Oak. The back four is The Ship Inn, Alma, Horseshoe and Barley Sheaf. In midfield are The Queen's Head, Prince of Wales and Black Bull, with The Cross Keys, Rose and Crown and Hare and Hounds up front. It's the local pub team.

Boy racer footballers: they're the torque of the town.

The book I'm reading about football training routines, I have to confess...I've skipped a couple of chapters.

Ayr United have placed Dan Druff on the transfer list. Word is Barnet are after him.

I've just scored my first senior goal. I play inside forward for Hillside Old Folks' Home.

My Grandmother plays for Manchester United. She's Nanny.

The blacksmith's shop took on a butchers' eleven in a real tasty encounter. Honestly, they were going at it hammer and tongue.

I bought a packet of Bic disposables and was shocked to find a former professional footballer, lurking on the inside. I thought, whey hey, it's Razor Ruddock.

Michael Owen asked me to mind the kids while he took the wife out for the night. Of course I agreed, but then he never answered the door when I turned up. Not that I'm surprised. He's been missing sitters for years.

My transfer to the trap door factory side: it's fallen through...

I was thinking about retiring, but changed my mind after a trip to Anfield. All through the game, the crowd were singing, work on, work on, with hope in your heart...

The girls from the sewing club football team: they're too good to go darn.

Wayne Rooney was subbed today. He borrowed twenty quid off Sir Alex till payday.

How do you stay cool at the footy? Stand next to a fan.

I was enjoying the Merseyside derby when this Liverpool fan got into a heated argument with an Everton supporter over whose team was best. Caught in the middle, I said, don't look at me, lads: I can see both sides...

Have you heard the news about the manager of the campanology society football team? He's been sacked for fielding a ringer.

An ecstatic youngster from the Ivory Coast made his debut for Liverpool then returned home to find his dad had been shot in a bungled burglary. He said, I hope you're not blaming me for this? His mother said, and why not? It was your idea to move us to Bootle, wasn't it?

I used to be Glenn Hoddle's chiropodist. I'll never forget the day his cultured left foot began lecturing me upon the mythology of ancient Greece.

Our star player's on a downward spiral: he's addicted to helter skelters.

They reckon Wenger's lost the dressing room. Well, tell him to go in through the front entrance, turn right down that long corridor and it's the third door on the left.

I can't believe we lost the cup tie against the Oxo factory. They made a right laughing stock out of us.

The referee awarded a penalty and my palms started crying. I blame the crowd for shouting, hand bawl!

We've just signed the great grandson of World War One fighter ace the Red Baron. Word on the grapevine is that he's brilliant in the air.

The millionaire toff's football club: they had too much for us.

I'm getting really excited: only three more Forest managers till Christmas.

In a fit of temper, I took a pair of scissors to my Subbuteo pitch, but was back playing again within the hour. It was a game of two halves.

Did you hear about the footballer who was stopped by police for using his mobile phone at the wheel? He said, give me a break: I am on the ring road.

I went to the Bernabéu with an old film director friend of mine, that Scott bloke who made Alien and Blade Runner. When the home side went one down, he ripped his seat up and threw it straight at celebrating Barcelona supporters in the stand below. I said to him, crikey, you're real mad Rid...

The penalty spot: I rubbed a bit of Freederm on it and, hey presto, it was gone!

Fergie lent Tom Cleverley his Mutiny on the Bounty DVD and the England international stupidly allowed his dog to chew it up. He said to his partner, mark my words: there will be a backlash over this!

AVB fielded a weakened team. He made them do a hundred push-ups and run a marathon then sent them straight out to play.

The under pressure manager sighed constantly with relief after claiming his first win in ten outings. He was clearly a man of phew words.

I bought tickets for the Theatre of Dreams. When I got there, it was a company of chocolate covered ice-creams on wooden sticks, giving a performance of King Lear.

It was a dead ball situation: the St John's ambulance man ran on the pitch and threw a coat over it.

That bloke down the club, the one who's half-feline-half-human: he's the kit man.

Vidiprinter manufacturing: it's a results business.

I've just seen this football player, holding a boot to his ear. I think he must have been listening to sole music.

Benitez bought a new dishwasher. He paid for it by Cech.

It's a standing joke at the club that, every time I venture into the opposition half, I get a nosebleed. Personally I blame their centre half...

Robbie Savage may have done well on Strictly Come Dancing, but he couldn't hack that tap dancing lark. He kept falling in the sink.

We've just drawn the fruit and veg' shop XI in the cup. Talk about a potential banana skin.

I just knew it: they beat us 2-1 after extra time, with the winner coming from a peach of a cross. Honestly, I'm as sick as a carrot...

We always travel to away matches by bus or car: never the twain.

Did you know that Hull City is the only football league club whose letters you can't colour in?

The dirtiest team I've ever seen? It has to be the chimney sweeps' eleven.

I've just cut my finger on a footballer: it was Billy Sharp.

The referee blew his whistle and all the players began fighting. It was kicking off time!

How many Peterborough United fans can you get in a Mini? Two in the back and two in the front: the entire supporters club.

The superstar striker, the one who played a full ninety minutes whilst recuperating from the flu: he didn't get a sniff.

I went to this match, where the wingers wore cruisers, battleships and aircraft carriers instead of boots: they were fleet-footed.

It's just been revealed that, for simplicity, perennial Black Country under achievers Wolves have agreed to change their name to Wolverhampton Wanderers Nil.

We've just signed a Jedi Knight on loan from Hoth United. He's not much cop, but still manages a goal every time he ventures into the opposition penalty area. It's Fluke Skywalker.

The ex-Magaluf barman in goal: I'm sick of him spilling shots...

What do you think to the new Italian football coach, the one who insists upon turning up at games in outrageous swimming costumes? It's Roberto Mankini.

I spotted Lineker, Wiggins and Tevez, having a group photo taken. I thought, ooh look, the good, the Brad and the ugly.

Bayern Munich's entire team were sent off yesterday: they went down to nein men...

When the weather forecast said gales, the last thing I expected was to see a Coronation street character named McIntyre and a footballer called Clichy, blowing down the street.

I can't believe they postponed the footy. It's just not on.

The gay XI football team: they've recorded five straight wins in a row.

Our 3-0 victory against the boys from the settee factory, I don't think I'd be exaggerating if I said it was comfortable.

That mannequin the boss insists upon playing out wide...it's just made a brilliant dummy run.

I must be losing it. I could have sworn it was Aston Villa on the tele, but then Martin Tyler threw a spanner in the works by announcing Ireland was offside...

Zenit Saint Petersburg striker Hulk is opening a shop in Cheltenham. Word is it's a greengrocers'.

We drew Crewe in the cup and lined up against a hundred and sixteen ratings from HMS Dauntless.

Kazimierz Deyna has been voted Legia Warsaw's best ever player. That is, according to Poles.

I said, I'm a Pumpey supporter. He said, don't you mean Pompey? I said, no, Pumpey: I follow the works' team from the running shoe factory.

The star player in the kindergarten football team: I've heard Man United are preparing a bib.

After weeks of anguish, the plumbers' football team are now mathematically safe from relegation. Check out the table: they've more than enough points in the bog.

I rattled the woodwork: I threatened to cut it down and chop it up for firewood.

Gerrard placed the ball in the quadrant then stepped back to make way for the bread van. It was delivering to the corner shop.

Rumour has it Fergie might play the promising on trial milkman this Saturday. That is, if he's got the bottle.

I always thought Jamie Carragher was real, but in a TV interview he finally admitted he was made up...

My mate knows absolutely nothing about football. He thought Sheffield Wednesday was a bank holiday.

One nil down against the shampoo factory, the hairdressers' full back lobbed a hopeful ball into the area...and the centre forward rose head and shoulders above the defence to equalise.

The debutant lined up with a 'toilets this way' placard attached to his back. He'd just been signed.

OK, so I'd had a few, but I'm telling you now: the kitchen furniture was talking to me. The chair said we'd finish third, the stool said we'd come second, and the table insisted we'd win it. I had to go with the latter. I mean, the table doesn't lie, does it...?

I went to the footy and was shocked to see visiting supporters, throwing missiles on the pitch. How on earth they managed to get their hands on a consignment of Iraqi army surplus, Russian made scuds is totally beyond me.

Joe Hart asked if I knew the way to Old Trafford. I shimmied then sent him the wrong way.

Fergie was contemplating signing a midfielder called Kieron but talked himself out of it. Apparently his injury record was Dyer.

I turned MOTD off in the end. I was sick of hearing Alan Hansen going on about how brilliant some dude called Rick Huvvery was...

Which Sunderland player once throttled a barrel of beer? Matthew Kill Gallon!

The manager had the players in a giant soup dish, filled with broth, and was moving the mix round anti-clockwise with a big spoon. He was bowl-stirring the squad.

David Blaine has taken up football but is currently suspended...in a block of ice, a hundred metres above the main stand.

I was on a flight over London when this bloke with a back-pack full of cash opened the door and jumped out, floating gently towards Loftus Road on a cloth canopy. The air hostess explained it was next season's parachute payment.

The boss has signed a new centre forward called Hale. He's alright but just lacking a bit of Pace...

I saw a frog, illegally parked outside Old Trafford. It got toad away.

Did you hear about the out of work football manager, who embarked upon a new career as a human cannonball? When he was sacked from that as well, he called a press conference, insisting, it's their loss: they'll never find anyone of the same calibre.

I was on a cruise, enjoying a game of deck football, when this big gust of wind blew the equipment overboard. I thought, we're two goals adrift.

Alex Oxlade-Chamberlain was sprinting round the track when Apollo, Poseidon and Zeus overtook him on the home straight. He was obviously in the lap of the Gods.

What would you get if you crossed a West Midlands football team with a plumbers' merchants? The Boggies!

I gave Shay Given a can of lager: it went straight down the keeper's throat.

What about the Carlisle United player, whose shot was so far off target, it clobbered a sheep in the field behind the ground? He hit the baa...

The highly successful Royal Oak darts team are turning their attentions to football. Landlord Jimmy Hardy has promised top flight action within five years...

I fell down a twenty foot hole in the penalty area. I was sent off for descent.

That Collymore bloke, the former footballer turned pundit, he stormed into my house last night and told me to shut up. I just stood there and looked at him in Stanned silence.

Our match against the Lamborghini XI: it was one way traffic.

I said, our goalie's got big ears. He said, don't you mean big hands? I said, no, big ears. He's kidnapped Noddy's best pal.

Arsenal: they're favourites for the sweet FA Cup.

Crowds were well down last season. But at least this year looks like getting off to a flyer: the manager is out posting little notes through people's letterboxes, reminding them we're still here!

I've got wooden legs and a rickety back, and I own my own football club. I'm the chair man.

My son has wooden legs and a rickety back as well, and deals drugs on street corners. He's the vice chair man.

The dental receptionists played the chiropodists receptionists in a local ladies league grudge match. They went for it tooth and nail.

Did you see Giggs on MOTD last night, reversing a National Express coach into the goalmouth? He was obviously parking the bus.

I went to the match and the visitors turned out in yellow and black hooped jerseys. I thought, whey hey, it's the Bee team.

There's this Dutch goalkeeper, who takes it out on his pet cat every time he has a bad game. It's Tim Cruel.

Arsene Wenger went to pay the bill in the restaurant. Guess what? He came up short.

Q: Who has played in every FA Cup Final for the past hundred years? A: The band.

I'm not saying footballers are overpaid, but when this footballer offered me his Jersey, the last thing I expected was to be made Governor of the Channel Islands...

Did you hear about the striker who hit the post? It hit him back!

Question for both Sheffield Wednesday's supporters: what is the most common form of owl in Great Britain? Answer: the teet!

I play Sunday league football for a team of insolvency experts. We aren't the most talented, but I have to say we're brilliant at closing down.

The price of diesel is getting so bad, I've actually missed a couple of away games recently. Two thousand quid it cost me yesterday to fill the tank up. Honestly, I rue the day I ever laid eyes on that Russian built T-34.

HOSPITAL PASS

Square ball? What? I thought they were meant to be round?

I scored with a curler. It was still in my hair from last night and the ball skimmed it on the way in...

The undertakers' XI are a decent side. In actual fact, they're excellent in the box.

What's green and wears glasses? A football pitch: I was lying about the glasses!

Did you hear about the out of form striker, whose new girlfriend dumped him after one date? His first touch let him down.

I was out hill-walking when I came across this character called Boaz, who claimed he played in goal for West Brom, before pushing me back down the slope again. He said, this is My Hill...

We played a team of mutes yesterday. We scored three times without reply.

Someone pinched the soap from the changing rooms. They made a clean getaway.

They stole the toilet seat as well. Neither the police nor the players have anything to go on.

I was on a cruise that sailed into an ocean of fizzy orange football matches. I thought, whey hey, Fanta sea football.

We were breezing it against the wind turbine factory football team. Then we blew it...

I said, I got those two free match tickets. He said, what for? I said, nothing...I got them for nothing.

Fergie disappeared up the tunnel. I said, where's he going? My mate said, for some gum. I said, for some gum? He said, yeah, it's Extra time.

Cristiano Ronaldo went to buy a new watch. The assistant said, Rolex? He said, of quartz.

What do you get if you cross an east London football team with an Everton international full back? Leyton Baines.

I play for the zoo football team: I'm the keeper.

We beat a big-headed team of bug-eyed aliens 23-0. We didn't half bring them down to earth.

Blackpool Pleasure Beach beat Alton Towers 3-1 yesterday. It was in the third round of the Fairs cup.

I entered the pub quiz with Gareth Bale. We got all our answers from under the table, courtesy of his educated left foot...

Did you know Henning Berg has two brothers, one named Ice and another called Chris De?

Ireland offered a first cap to Newcastle defender Col O'Ccini.

When he turned them down, they turned their attentions to up-and-coming American star, Phil O'Delphia...

The camera zoomed in on Arsene Wenger, sitting in between Collymore and Petrov. I thought, ooh look, he's been sent to the Stans...

I fell in love with a girl who supported Spartak Moscow. I was going to ask her to marry me, but didn't want to Russia.

We need to be careful against the motor mechanics team in the cup this weekend. The boss had them watched and reckons that, when the going gets tough, they don't half know how to step up a gear.

Unlike the road workers' XI: they wouldn't have a clue how to dig themselves out of a hole.

Can you believe a team of goats actually won the Premier League? Who said you can't win anything with kids?

I wouldn't say we're involved in a relegation dogfight. But we're that far behind, we need snookers.

South African soccer triumphs: I've got the Boks' set.

The subject of intense transfer scrutiny, Demba Ba was bound and gagged in the club boiler room. Like the manager said, he's going nowhere...

Did you see the chickens FA Cup final last night? It was real hen to hen stuff.

I've heard that, when Colchester enquired about Scott Parker recently, all his agent did throughout the meeting was scribble endless pictures of fake bullets. Needless to say, the U's drew a blank...

What did the referee say when he sent off the Middle Eastern footballer? It's an oily bath for you, my lad!

The head-postmaster, the one who plays centre half for us on Sundays: he was sent off for stamping...

Commentary: And it's Lescott to Tevez. Tevez returns the ball to Lescott, who passes it back to Tevez. Tevez beats three, plays a one two with Lescott, and then blasts the ball in to the net, before being hugged stupid by the ecstatic Lescott. Tevez and Lescott...it's a beautiful game.

The head-postmaster, the one who plays centre half for us on Sundays: he was sent off for stamping...

I walked out on Alcoholics Anonymous FC when they admitted they couldn't guarantee me thirst team football.

Och aye the noo, as star player of the Glasgow grapplers, I cannae wait for tomorrow's footy match against our fiercest rivals, the Sassenach wrestlers XI...otherwise known as the hold enemy.

We give every spectator a meat pie upon admission: we're a feeder club.

I went to the big match the day after Christmas and a mass brawl broke out in the penalty area. Not that anyone was surprised. After all, it was Boxing Day.

Plymouth Argyle is the only side I know who do a lap of honour when they get a corner.

Fergie asked Michael Carrick if he could count on him. Carrick said, of course, and so Fergie jumped on his back and went, one, two, three, four, five...

I was getting ready to defend a corner when this car went past, blaring its horn. I was pipped at the post.

Despite another heavy defeat, the manager can still claim to have the crowd behind him. They chased him through the back streets and all the way home...

The grocers' football team: as soon as they go a goal up, they shut up shop.

What would you get if you crossed a racing driver with a Māori war chant, Patrick Swayze's co-star in Ghost and the fat content of a large cream cake? Hamilton Haka Demi Cals!

I went on an away day to Liverpool and it started raining ships. I thought, nice weather for docks.

Cliff Richard's sponsored football team are something else. Honestly, we were chasing Shadows half the match.

Did you hear about the alcoholic's football team? They went out in the forty-third round.

I parked my car at the foot of the tunnel. I was booked for obstruction.

Welbeck didn't half get angry with himself when he missed an open goal. Talk about red missed!

The town criers' society has entered a team in the FA Cup. Call me naive if you like, but I reckon they're in with a shout...

Lost at home? I thought, what's all that about? How can anyone get lost in their own manor...?

I couldn't believe it when I saw a car, eating the pitch. It was Honda-soil-eating.

Word is David Beckham was bitterly disappointed with movie blockbuster, Zulu. Expecting wall-to-wall action, all he got was two hours about a trainee toilet attendant at Chester Zoo.

Did you hear about the footballer who made a fortune from his investment in a savoury potato cakes company and then just frittered it all away...?

I was at Stamford Bridge when Gareth Bale went down a bit too easily. The crowd shouted, give him an Oscar! Abramovich took this one step further, gifting him the club's Brazilian attacking midfielder.

Sergio Agüero was driving home in his new Lamborghini when he suddenly broke down. He sobbed, I can't stand the pressure anymore...

The insects were losing 72-0 against the ants when the centipede goalkeeper finally clomped on to the field. He'd only just got his boots on.

I was driving past United's training ground when I spotted this bloke, nicking the gates. I didn't say anything to him: I didn't want him to take a fence.

When Derby County were relegated from the Premier League, I nailed my season ticket to a tree in the middle of the moors. I went back a few days later and someone had nicked the nail.

I used to be a part-time pro' for KP: it was OK, but the pay was peanuts.

Arsene Wenger gave a debut to a Maltese international. He was a small ball of honeycomb, coated in milk chocolate.

I've just seen the club chairman on his way out of the craft shop, carrying a roll of flexible leaf fibre, the same roll of flexible leaf fibre that has been rumoured to have applied for the current managerial vacancy. Who'd have thought it, a club like ours, attracting the likes of Raffia Benitez...?

Tom Daley had a trial with League Two side Oxford United. First match, he was booked for diving.

I used to play for Harry Potter's football team. But then he let me go. Now I'm back for a second spell...working my magic.

After a training ground collision, Aaron Lennon went to the surgery, complaining of double vision. He remarked later that Doctor Hourihane and Doctor Hourihane couldn't have been more understanding.

I've just seen Fernando Torres, punching a bench in the park. I knew he'd hit form sooner or later.

The match started at eight instead of quarter to, and when it did, all I could hear was the sound of chickens, laying eggs. It was a late cluck off.

I understand where Theo Walcott was coming from when he tweeted online that Wenger played him out of position last night. He was lining up at St James' Park, while the match was kicking off at the Emirates.

Postman Pat was short-cutting across the pitch when the ball hit his mail sack and then bobbled over the line. It went in off the post.

What do you get if you cross a footballer with a box of washing powder? Robin Van Persil.

I went to watch the writers and artists XI play but came away unimpressed. No creativity.

On a visit to Cadbury's World, Nottingham Forest striker Billy Sharp dove bravely into a vat of chocolate to save a lady who had slipped then fallen in. Witnessing her husband, hauling the woman to safety, his wife began to sing, to the tune of Paper Lace, Billy, don't be an Aero...

I see our new Hawaiian centre half has cried off again. Apparently he's got aloha back injury.

My mate said, how do you fancy an away day in Helsinki? I said, sounds cool.

I've just had a very Frank exchange with some footballer who said he could lamp a ball hard.

We only just scraped through against the bike shop XI. They didn't half put in a late Raleigh.

There's this team up north where, if a player injures a leg, they simply remove it and replace it with a brand new one. It's Bolt-on Wanderers.

I used to get picked on by this footballer. It was Bully Bremner.

How about the big fight between the rugby field and the football field? According to form, it was a right pitched battle.

Word is Fergie is contemplating playing Usain Bolt in Manchester United's charity match against Real Madrid legends and all because he runs like the wind. I say, go on, Sir Alex, follow your instincts: grant him a gust appearance.

The classical composers' association football team: they've just secured Bach to Bach victories.

I've just stolen the bottom third of all the football league tables in the world. I've got relegation form.

The angels XI football team...take it from me, they're up there!

I couldn't believe it when I won free tickets to see W Ham. George Michael, what a performer!

What would you get if you crossed Terry Yorath's daughter with a WBA supporter and Aston Villa's star player? Gabby Ag-Boing Lahore!

I've just seen this sergeant major, tearing a strip off a football field. I thought, ooh look, a pitch inspection.

Sportsflash: Play was halted at White Hart Lane today when a dozen cows found their way on to the field and trampled the goalkeeper underfoot. The referee stopped play immediately, as you would expect with a herd injury...

We've just signed a player with a very unusual surname: Firstpintofthenight. He's quite good actually, but doesn't half go down easy.

I arrived at the turnstyle and slapped fifty quid on the counter. I said, two, please. The cashier said, what do you want: strikers or defenders?

I've watched every Preston North End game, home and away, since 11th February, 1989, which, purely by coincidence, was the first time the Australian programme, set in Summer Bay, was broadcast. And what do you think my favourite soap is? It's Emmerdale, of course!

We agreed to play the zombies in a challenge match. But never again, I can tell you. 10-0 we were beating them...then they came back from the dead.

The rubber boot factory team: they've been wellygated.

When Wycombe went behind in the first minute, this bloke's dog did a triple salco down the steps then hopped back up again on its hind legs. I said, what's it do when Wycombe score? He said, I don't know. I've only had it two years.

I asked my mate what the record attendance was for a football match in England. He said, eighty-four thousand, five hundred and sixty-nine: Manchester City versus Stoke City at Maine Road on the third of March, nineteen thirty-four. I said, alright then, big head, name them...

Shelvey lined up for kick-off, holding a piece of rope with handles. The ref said, what's all this about, Jonjo? He said, the gaffer's made me the skipper for the day.

Have you heard who we've signed? Gordon Bennett!

I went to watch LA Galaxy and this cowboy asked me to lend him a twenty dollars. I think it was Skint Eastwood.

I've just been awarded my coaching badges. If you need me, you'll find me driving the number 23 bus.

We played against a team in Robin Hood costumes yesterday. They weren't brilliant, but I'll tell you what: their big, fat, bald-headed centre forward doesn't half know how to Tuck them away...

The England team visited an orphanage in South Africa yesterday. It was heart warming to put a smile on the faces of people who constantly struggle and have virtually no hope...said little Albert Owusu, aged 7.

One on one with the keeper, with a minute to go, I feinted left...a bucket of cold water and a dose of smelling salts soon sorted me out.

Where did Cristiano Ronaldo sign his new, eight million pounds per year contract? At the bottom!

I wasn't impressed when the coach tried showing me how to lay the ball off. I said, why should I be the one who makes the poor little windbag redundant?

Heskey: when he goes down, you can guarantee he'll make Emile of it.

It's the season's Final day. Not that it means anything to us. We went out in the first round.

I said to the wife, I got sent off today. She said, what for? I said, for the remaining thirty-three minutes.

When David Beckham arrived back off holiday, his IPhone sprouted wings and started flying round the room. He'd left it in airplane mode.

I went to watch Dagenham and there was this bloke in the crowd, wearing a green cap, green shirt, green shorts and green socks, who wouldn't stop singing, ging-gang-goolie-goolie-goolie-goolie-whatcha, ging-gang-goo, ging-gang-goo. I can't say for certain, but I think he was a scout.

Did you hear about the footballer who was addicted to online gambling? He spent all day, every day, hanging upside down on the washing line, talking to the bookies.

I asked this Milwall fan about 1960's East End mob rule. He said it was all the Krays.

My mate rang. He said, have you heard we've just signed John McEnroe? I said, you cannot be serious!

Did you see that player on MOTD, walking off the field, covered in ground baking spices: he'd been nutmegged.

After a brilliant start to the season, the scientists' footy team is plummeting down the league. It's the manager I feel sorry for: he isn't half under the microscope.

INTERNATIONAL CLEARANCE

I bumped into Giorgos Karagounis on a visit to Athens. He said, Αθήνα είναι πραγματικά όμορφη στο καλοκαίρι. I just ignored him: it was all Greek to me.

As the promotion race hots-up, it's Wolves who are leading the pack...now that is a joke!

We've just signed a really ugly Colombian striker. Honestly, he's a right foul cow...

I was a promising young footballer until I started eating meat pies. Then it all went pear-shaped.

Where do the world's most enthusiastic football supporters come from, the ones with the very sore hands? It's got to be Clapham!

I've just watched a game between two rival teams of comedians. Talk about a funny old game.

What do you call an Aston Villa footballer with a car on his head? Kia Ron Clark!

Pep Guardiola was clean shaven. Next time I looked, he had a big beard and moustache. He was in the technical hairier.

Did you hear about the wasp attacking midfielder? It shot and stung the goalkeeper's palms.

I've just seen a chicken, taking a throw in. The referee blew for a fowl...

Asked about tomorrow's big FA Cup tie, the manager of the mute society replied, we'll do our talking on the pitch...

All the players fetched their dogs to the game. I thought, ooh look, the wags.

We've just been hammered 6-1 by HMP Strangeways. It's fair to say we didn't do ourselves justice.

I went to the footy and there was this sign saying, Howay fans only. I thought, they've spelled that wrong. But I was mistaken. When I got inside, it was full of Geordies, singing Toon songs...

Our match against the lads from the charcoal factory: if you ask me, we just shaded it.

We've just signed a Swede. Rumour has it we're signing a turnip next and then an onion.

There's this bloke going round, making a career from pretending he's that big-eared ex-England striker, the one who makes a living presenting Match of the Day. It's Gary Mimicker.

I said, that was a nice height for the keeper. He said, what was? I said, six-foot four.

What's the difference between the Spice Girls and Sir Alex? Sir Alex still plays Giggs.

The home side formed up wearing expensive jewellery pieces: the manager was playing a diamond formation.

Apparently Sven-Göran Eriksson is taking time out. His new girlfriend is an alarm clock.

I asked this ventilation engineer who he supported. He said, I'm an extractor fan...

We really struggled against the casino XI: the croupier centre half was magnificent. Honestly, he dealt with everything we threw at him.

The Irish football manager offered boxing champ David Haye's trainer a first cap.

Someone had told him it only takes a second to score a goal.

What would you get if you crossed Leeds United's goalkeeper with a baked potato? Kenny Jacket.

I'm on tele next week, exposing corrupt referees: I'm a whistleblower.

Some bloke called Cropper scored the winner in the Coronation Street versus Eastenders football challenge. It was Roy of the Rovers stuff.

Why did the footballer turn out in his swimming trunks? Because the boss told him to play down the channels.

The Doors fan club formed a football team. Training went well and optimism was high...until the star striker picked up a knock.

I've just seen our manager, chatting with Jack Wilshire in the bathroom showroom. I think he was tapping him up.

The decision to sign a couple of players from the allergy clinic never really paid off. Not that I'm surprised. I always thought it was a bit rash.

I went to watch Liverpool play Blyth Spartans and couldn't believe it when the referee proposed to a girl in the crowd. But then I suppose that's the romance of the cup.

Javier Hernández has a new soft perm: it's a Mexican wave.

Tombstone FC played Dodge City in a hugely anticipated grudge match. Grudge match? I've never seen anything like it: talk about all guns blazing...

I couldn't believe it when the cup pitched us against a team made up of small, freshwater fish. Talk about minnows.

Who is John Travolta's favourite international football team? Greece!

The pitch was three feet deep in water and overflowing with pieces of short-cut wood. I thought, ooh look, it's water-logged.

According to the pundits, we don't have a problem on paper. What worries me is we're playing on grass.

I got absolutely smashed at this Chelsea player's housewarming party. It's the last time you'll catch me drinking at Demba's bar.

Our new signing was curled into a ball in the midfield area, repeatedly performing head over heels gymnastic movements. He was on a rolling contract.

In the post-match interview, a player was asked to comment upon his misplaced pass that led to the decisive third goal. He said, look, don't just blame me. I wasn't the only one out there. Other players made mistakes as well, you know. But then I don't suppose you noticed that, did you? No, of course you didn't. And am I surprised? Hardly, and I'll tell you for why: because you've always had it in for me, haven't you? You've had it in for me from day one. What's up? Are you jealous because I'm on a hundred grand a week and you're struggling to pay the gas bill? You're pathetic, always have been. Not that I'm telling you anything you don't already know. Your wife probably tells you the same every day of the week. Why not try asking our centre half about how he missed that cross, allowing United to nip in and equalise? If he'd been on his game, it would never have happened. Or our centre forward? He played miles worse than I did. He missed two chances in the first five minutes alone. Why don't you ask him about what he could have done differently? Honestly, he couldn't hit a barn door with that left foot of his. It makes me wonder what the gaffer was thinking about, signing him in the first place: him and the rest of the rubbish out there tonight. None of them are fit to lace my boots and that's a fact.

Anyway, look, let's set things straight, shall we? Just for the record, I'll have you know I was fouled from behind a split second before I went to pass. Their player nearly took my legs off. But then I don't suppose you saw that either, did you? No, I didn't think so. Your type never do, do you? You think you're experts, but the truth is you know nothing. And, when I say nothing, I mean nothing. My three-year old son has more idea about the game than you ever will. If I were you, I think I'd pack it all in, mate. Go and get a job as a carpenter, or sweeping the streets, or something. You'd be of more use. What are you anyway, blind? You want to get your eyes seen to if you ask me, you and the ref, and his pathetic linesmen. I can recommend a good optician if you want. Mind you, I don't think I'll bother. You're that short-sighted, you'd never find it. Anyway, stick your interview where the sun doesn't shine. Find someone else to answer your smarmy questions, because I've had it with you. Right, I'm off for a shower and, if there aren't any towels left, I'll want to know why. Comprende...? When he'd gone, the producer asked the interviewer what all that was about. He said, oh, I wouldn't worry about him: he's just a defensive midfielder...

He interviewed another player next, who punched him straight on the nose: it was an attacking midfielder.

And then another that took off right in front of him: the flying winger.

Not forgetting the defender in knee length shorts, button-down shirt and big, leather boots: the old fashioned centre half.

Arsene Wenger thought Salford Van Hire was a Dutch international striker...

The apprentice plumber we took a gamble on, he scored the winner on his debut. The ball arrived at his feet and he just tapped it in.

I've signed my pooch on for the dog's footy team. He made his debut yesterday and scored the whining goal...

Signing for cardigan factory football team was the best move I've ever made. We're such a tight knit squad.

Why did the footballer turn out with a chemist's shop on each foot? Because they were his new Boots.

On a related subject, have you heard they've stopped selling Red Bull in boots? It leaks out of the lace holes.

I was watching this game in the local park when one of the players hit a kangaroo on the head with the ball. They had jumpers for goalposts.

We're facing a difficult away trip to the north-west this weekend: the M6 is closed, so we'll have to travel north up the M1 then cut across the M62, past the Little House on the Prairie, and down the M60 towards Manchester Airport...

Steve McClaren sold his PC and bought a Mac. He said at least it keeps him dry in the rain without the need for a brolly.

When David Beckham signed for LA Galaxy, a reporter asked him if he'd ever been abroad before arriving in America. He replied, no, mister, I ain't never been a woman...

I thought the boss was barking mad when he played a Dalmatian dog up front in last week's big derby. Hats off to him, though: with a minute left, it sniffed out a rare opportunity and nipped through to bag the winner...

Thieves broke into the Emirates last night and stole all the cups. Apparently the canteen lady is livid.

A second break-in has now been reported at the Emirates. Thieves got in through a window and completely emptied the trophy room. Police are looking for someone with a rolled-up, red and white carpet.

Frank Lampard couldn't believe when the waiter fetched him a glass of smiling pop. He said, what's this? The waiter said, it's your happy Tizer.

I couldn't believe it when Cardiff announced their new centre half was a three-bedroomed, semi-detached...but it did bring a whole new meaning to the term house clearance!

We've just signed a former traffic warden. The gaffer reckons he's in fine fettle.

Did you know there used to be a footballer who was named after the abbreviated name of a British Army Regiment? It was REME Moses.

I said, Liverpool's back four were under the cush yesterday. He said, don't you mean cosh? I said, no, cush: I popped in DFS and they were all asleep on the sofa.

Net profits are down: we're sending the goalposts back.

All square with a minute to go, I had the perfect opportunity to win it against a stubborn brickies XI when we were awarded a free kick on the edge of the area. I hit the wall.

I've converted my loft into a shrine to Crystal Palace. But the wife isn't happy. She thinks I'm fan-attic-al.

A long strip of white chalk, painted on grass, just shouted cheerio to me. I think it was the bye line.

Did you see that programme last night, the one about the treatment of football players, suffering from a clash of heads? Stunning.

I'm not saying our keeper's getting a bit long in the tooth, but he made his debut against Royal Engineers.

Can you believe my next door neighbour was banging my door down at three in the morning? It was a good job I was still up, practising with the lads from the Sheffield Wednesday band.

My career's definitely on the up: I've just been linked with a move to the rope and chain XI...

Rooney ran on the field, drew a pistol and aimed it with menace. Fergie took the flak for it, explaining it was him who told him to hold the ball up.

Why does Brendan Rodgers insist upon driving the Liverpool squad round in circles all day? Because everyone keeps telling him they're a team in transition.

I couldn't believe it when our winger was upended by a main battle tank: talk about a bad Challenger.

The chap holding up the board, indicating three added minutes, he doesn't look to be in a very good mood. I think it must be the fourth Huff-icial.

We've just won a fair play award: everyone in the team has long, blond hair.

The peasants' football team lost 46-0 to the squires. Poor defending was the cause.

I arrived at the footy and thought, oh, no! The visitors were lined up on the half way line, picking their noses. It was our bogey team.

Did you hear about the footballer who took a flag on a stick and a quadrant of turf home with him? He'd won a corner.

I play Sunday league football for the Swan Vestas factory XI. We're not a bad side really: we're just lacking a couple of strikers.

Last week, I was nominated man of the match...

That mass murderer, the one who was going round, clobbering victims with a toastie machine, Vinnie Jones is starring in the lead role of a film about his life. Tefal Weapon is released in the summer.

Did you know there's a Premiership manager who keeps a daily record of toilet activity? It's Tony Pooh List.

I love football and knew I'd end up getting Sky in the end: my roof blew off.

A streaker ran on the field during the women's FA Cup Final. The shout went up, man on!

I bumped into this footballer who couldn't stop laughing: it was Wilfried Haha.

Fergie went to the doctors complaining that, every time he wins a trophy, he comes out in a sweat and suffers abnormally high body temperatures. Wenger raised an eyebrow when he heard. He said he had it once...but it was a very long time ago.

I went to this match the other day and all the players were spark out in the centre circle. It was a knockout competition.

We completely outplayed the yanks from the base. To be fair, they weren't bad defensively: they just didn't get enough buddies forward.

The new inside forward we signed from HJK Helsinki, boy-oh-boy, does he know how to Finnish...

Why was Nemanja Vidic hanging upside down from the ceiling? Because he'd been suspended.

No wonder the match is off. It's been raining cats and dogs all day. In fact, I've just trod in a poodle.

Roy Hodgson was less than impressed when he was charged a fortune for new tyres on his 4X4. He said it was highway rubbery.

I was watching this old American detective series, set in Hawaii, and think one of the cops must have been a former referee. All the way through, his colleague kept saying, book him, Danno...

As the vets' football team's number one fan, I had such high hopes when we were drawn away at Aldershot Town in the 1st round of the FA Cup. I couldn't believe it when we went out without a whimper.

We didn't half get stuck in last night: the pitch we played on was a right quagmire.

When Michael Owen developed a tickly cough, the wife rubbed his chest with Vic. It eased the cough, but he came out in an awful rash from his stubbly chin.

She packed Michael straight off to bed afterwards. When he got up, next morning, he'd sprouted four legs, pointed ears, and had a thick mane of hair on the back of his neck. When the wife asked if he was feeling better, he said, not bad. I'm just a bit horse, that's all.

I've just been tackled by a box of washing powder: it was an Aerial challenge.

Did you know Maradona had a brother called Prima?

When the Reds trotted down the tunnel, draped in tinsel and baubles, I thought, whey hey, it's the Christmas tree formation.

The team of former army officers: they've just reached their first Major final...

I've heard Fernando Torres is attracting interest from the Far East. Word on the grapevine is that it's Grimsby Town.

The crossbar fell out with the post. It was all down to goal difference.

Arteta misplaced his pass, put off by the non-stop clunking of pistons. It was coming from Steven Gerrard's engine room.

I bet you didn't know there's this team playing in the Italian league made up exclusively of players from the local Pampers factory: it's Nappyli.

The ball smacked me on the backside, ouch! It was a real pile driver!

BICYCLE KICK

We've just signed a player on a short-term contract from the local asylum. He's out on loon.

I went to watch Liverpool play and there was this seven foot bloke, walking round the pitch in a suit of armour, speaking with a French accent. It was another big European knight at Anfield.

We were playing the Matchbox cars enthusiasts. With a minute to go, it was all square: then I picked up this loose ball and Dinky'd it over the keeper...

I was a bit bemused when we gave a debut to Uri Geller. Credit where credit's due, mind: he did bend in a brilliant winner.

So this bloke said, name me the best coach in the world. I said, is it National Express?

The reporter who conducts Steven Gerrard and Jamie Carragher's post-match interviews, I bet you didn't know it was an animated cow called Ermentrude from classic BBC children's programme, Magic Roundabout. Next time they're on, pay close attention and you'll hear them going, yeah, definitely, you know Errrrmmm...

I think Wayne Rooney's turning into a shark: he's going fin on top.

All the players were roasting their hands over an electric fire in the centre circle: they were warming up.

David Beckham went into this plant hire shop? He said, can I rent two yuccas and an aloe vera till a week on Sunday?

What do you get if you cross a ship's company with an Egyptian seaport? Crew Alexandria!

I've just seen a mouse, disappearing inside Glen Johnson's shorts. Talk about squeaky-bum time.

Did you hear the one about the drug addict footballer? He kept giving away needle-less free kicks.

Howard Webb gave me a lift in his new car. I said, what's that fancy button on the dash, Howard? He said, oh, that: it's just my trip recorder...

On a visit to the Etihad, I spotted this player, abseiling up and down the main stand, not once, not twice, but numerous times in rapid succession. I thought, ooh look, it's Yo-Yo Touré.

I led Leeds United fans in a Marching On Together sing-song for the full ninety minutes. Former player Peter Lorimer said it was a club record.

Our new director of football: it's Steven Spielberg.

Did you hear about the misfiring striker who skied his shot and took down a passing satellite...?

The Sunday league side I play for, we're up against a team of table-topping ruler salesmen next week. I can't wait to see how we measure up.

I was invited to submit a couple of football related topics for discussion online. Unfortunately I've nothing forum.

Fergie was photographed putting Evra, Jones, Ferdinand and Rafael in a suitcase. General consensus is that he was packing the defence.

If you crossed a South Wales football team with a broken down vehicle, what would you get? Car Duff City!

This bloke standing next to me at the match said, what can you tell me about the striker with the flaming boots? I said, not much: I just know he's on fire.

I went to Reading: I took my own book!

That Titanic movie is a right load of twaddle. The bit where Jack and Rose are standing on the bow of the ship against the background of a crimson sky? It was the year Barnsley won the FA cup, remember, and I've seen the footage: everyone knows the world was still in black and white in 1912.

Football match tonight: Choristers Verses Poets.

Aled Jones got the winner: he wasn't half on song.

On a tour of Anfield, I asked the guide what the big plank of wood was in the corridor. He said it was the board.

Referee Martin Atkinson dropped his watch outside Old Trafford. Just leaving for home, Fergie immediately put his foot down, aiming straight for it. I thought, whey hey, he's running the clock down...

I've just heard Carlton Cole has bought another dog to go with the one he got last week. He bought it second hound.

We've just been beaten by a team of former jockeys. That said, they didn't half ride their luck.

Last time Rotherham won anything, the score was printed in Roman numerals.

I went to Hawaii and was staggered how many people mentioned Scottish side, Alloa.

The community hall near me was booked by sixty-eight angry football pitches for their annual dance night. It was a cross field ball.

Michael Laudrup: all he does is Swansea around all day.

John Terry hit the ball into space. It was last seen passing Mars in the direction of constellation Alpha Centauri.

I put Crippen clean through on goal. Talk about a killer pass.

We never win on the road: the tarmac doesn't suit our favourite studs.

Our manager keeps a chart of his club sponsored car, including daily mileage. It's his auto graph.

I hate to tell you, but the wife had a near death experience last night: she only started Hoovering while the football was on.

I went to my first Bundesliga game this weekend. Before kick-off, each of the players picked up this little midfielder and wobbled him round a bit. Sitting next to me was Franz, who explained it was the pre-match Hans shake...

Who's the best player? Lionel Messi? Or Bobby Zamora? It's no contest, really. Zamora has two England caps, while Messi doesn't have any.

How many footballers can you get in a breadbin? A breadbinful!

I went to the match and all the players were spinning round like tops. I think it had something to do with the manager's squad rotation policy.

Did you hear about the Irishman who thought Manual Labour was a Spanish international footballer?

The bluebottles' first ever international squad was named yesterday and the manager was absolutely slated over his selection. He didn't pick any goalkeepers. He didn't pick any full backs. He didn't pick any centre halves. He didn't pick any midfielders. He didn't pick any or forwards. All he picked was wing backs.

I'm in the same class as Messi. Well, I used to be. We both went to the same High School in Argentina.

Why was John Terry wearing an oil painting instead of an armband? Because he wears his art on his sleeve.

I've heard Liverpool have resigned Barry Venison: he wasn't deer.

Our new manager, the former pizza shop boss, the fans are starting to grow impatient: they think it's time he delivered...

I stopped off for fish and chips and was shocked to discover the shop had been bought out by one of FIFA's top dignitaries. It was Sepp Batter.

We have a match on Shrove Tuesday: the toss is at three o'clock.

I was at the airport and spotted Arsene Wenger reading this French footballer's autobiography. Les Misérables, he sounds like a right manic depressive to me...

Which football ground has the most grass? Turf More.

The squaddies football team remain in the bottom four after a goalless draw: it's as you were.

I said, new signing, Penny Farthing, scored a brilliant late winner. He said, don't tell me: it was a bicycle kick? I said, actually, no, it was a twenty-five yard pile-driver.

Our new winger, the one who was in the paper recently for buying two terraced houses, he's definitely got that extra yard...

Rooney went down injured and this bottle of orange Fanta ran on to tend him. The bloke in the seat next to me said, who the heck is that? I said, don't worry, it's just the Fizzio...

Petr Cech, Joe Hart, Robert Green, Wojciech Szczesny and David de Gea all got on the same bus as me. I said to the driver, I didn't know it was a goalkeeping coach.

I run a football team of high-ranking army officers. I'm the General Manager.

We went to the last match of the season in seventies fancy dress, but were refused entry on health and safety grounds. The steward said, sorry, lads, no flares...

My first game in charge of the barbers' shop football team and the lads were four down by half time. Honestly, I didn't half give them the hairdryer treatment.

Overweight footballers: they don't half make a meal of it.

I went to a game between two teams of women, all wearing black habits and headdresses. It was a Nun league match.

For the first time in years, Wenger's finally got his name on the cup. It's got a big tea stain round the rim and says: Arsene, best dad in the world.

Have you ever seen an executive box? I have: he lost on points over ten rounds.

I couldn't believe it when David Moyes turned up to view my collection of old vinyl. He said, let's have a Decca...

Defoe brought this seven year old kid down on his chest then blasted him over the bar. I thought, ooh look, a ball boy.

The big argument over whether the pitch was waterlogged or not, it spilled over on to the terraces.

I almost choked on my beer when I read that one in three former footballers is an alcoholic. Staggering.

Our match against the Baywatch XI: it's been called Hoff.

When Carlisle's floodlights failed, the club sent for a local egg famer, who promptly turned up with six hundred birds. Sure enough, within a couple of minutes, the game was back on again. When asked how he did it, he replied, many hens make lights work...

I went to the footy, and there was this bloke being whipped on the touchline. I thought, whey hey, a corner flog.

My mate said, only another six hours and we'll be in Hartlepool. I said, sorry, can you repeat that? I was miles away...

Stylianos Giannakopoulos signed for Borussia Mönchengladbach: it took the ref ten minutes to book him.

I went to Alton Towers and spent the day with Sam Allardyce, Mick McCarthy and Alex McLeish. Talk about managerial merry-go-round.

We played a pre-season friendly against this team made up of bottles of Lucozade Sport: we were taking on fluids.

In a charity football match to celebrate forty years of the Italian Job, Michael Caine turned on a sixpence, beat three defenders and blasted home the winner...and all with just five Minis left on the clock.

Graham Taylor went to see new Steven Spielberg film, Lincoln, but left early when he wasn't mentioned once.

I went to this Blue Square Bet Premier League match: a Smurf scored the winner.

Did you hear about the footballer who went straight to the game after filming his latest after shave advert? The referee scent him off.

Howard Webb: he's been nominated for the Booker Prize.

I went to a match between two teams of rival Ford motor cars. Talk about football Focus.

Manchester City have signed a pre-contract agreement with Peppa Pig: they're just waiting for the oink to dry.

It's been reported that Chelsea are in negotiations to sign Galatasaray's promising teenage winger: they're talking Turkey.

Man United's gates are the best in the Premier League. The latest ones are twelve foot tall, manufactured from sheet metal and painted bright red.

The ex-television salesman we've got playing for us, he doesn't half know how to turn it on...

I'm a bit disappointed with our new centre forward. He's never reached the heights he did at Kathmandu United.

There's a rumour going round that David Blaine is to become the new owner of Walsall. Not that I'm under any illusions...

Vinnie Jones discovered a stranger in his bedroom. He took him down.

I saw David Moyes in B&Q, buying a new toilet. It was nothing fancy, just bog standard.

What do you get if you cross an animated sheep with the correct answer and a perpendicular screwdriver? Shaun Right Phillips!

I was caught climbing over the wall at Donny Rovers: the stewards grabbed me by the scruff of the neck and made me go back in and watch the last half hour.

John Terry was driving down the road and spotted a sign on the back of this van, which said: Mob: 07741 897103. So he rang the number for a laugh. Ten minutes later, he had the Sicilian Mafia camped out on his doorstep.

There was this whistling, mouse-like creature, lying flat-out in the penalty area, with the keeper, crying his eyes out. I thought, oh no, he's dropped another Clanger.

I went to a cup game between the Irish and Scottish malt whisky associations: it was the White Horse final.

Stevie Wonder made a guest appearance for Rovers last Saturday. He played an absolute blinder.

Then there was the footballer, who discovered a hedgehog, floating in his pint. He said, this has been spiked.

A fight broke out in our match against the purse factory XI. Nothing serious: just handbags.

I have to say I'm fantastic in the middle of the park: it's just the swings that get in the way.

After another heavy defeat, the manager of the vampires football team said, we need fresh blood...

I said, what's that football agent doing here? He said, oh, him: he's just here to make up the numbers.

We took the lead at Goodison Park with a shot from twenty-three yards, two feet, six and a half inches...that is, according to the away goals ruler.

.

There was this game taking place at the leisure centre, where all the players had been diagnosed with the Norovirus: it was sicks-a-side.

I've been capped seventy-five times now. My knees are in a dreadful mess...

The cartoonists' club challenged the caricature society to a game of football: it was a draw.

They played the drill company next: this time it was a bore-draw.

I've just seen the gaffer on his way into the ground with Monopoly under one arm and Kerplunk under the other. I thought, ooh look, two games in hand.

Luton Town fans: they've a never say die Hatter-tude.

I put twenty quid on the solo musicians' team in football's celebrity world cup. Typical, they didn't even make the group stages.

Sportsflash: The former takeaway owner, making his Stevenage debut, he's just chipped in a brilliant winner...

Mark Lawrenson on MOTD doesn't half confuse me. Last night, he was on about two players, who went for the same ball. I thought, how many balls are there supposed to be...?

I caught my son, stamping on the Spanish Subbuteo team I'd just bought him. He said he was on an international break.

Our strikers had a hundred and sixteen shots in the first ten minutes. How they managed to smuggle ten bottles of Jägerbomb on to the field of play is anyone's guess.

RAIN ROO KNEE

I've just been made manager of the month. I'm so proud to be the gaffer at January United.

We're playing a team of zombies in a friendly tomorrow night. We're live on Sky Sports. But they're not...

Van Persie volleyed in a jar of humbugs: it was the sweetest of strikes.

I went on an away day to Spurs and thought I'd treat myself by booking in at the Ritz. Imagine my disappointment when I ended up spending the night in a box of salted crackers.

Tom Thumb made his City debut last weekend, but then threw a tantrum when he was substituted. If you ask me, it's time he grew up a bit.

Liverpool's pre-season friendly against the Rag Trade XI: it's being held behind clothed doors.

The ex-pro boxers association entered a team in the FA Cup: they got knocked out in the first round.

My favourite position is sweeper. I've just signed for West Broom.

I was disappointed with my seven-year old son's debut match. Schoolboy defending doesn't come into it.

Apparently Theo Walcott has pulled a muscle. It doesn't make sense to me: he can have any woman he wants and chooses to date a slimy mollusc.

Commentary: And tonight's football comes from the Emirates, where Arsenal entertain Origami United in the third round of the cup. We'll be there live as the action unfolds...

I started out my career in the Grenadier Guards football team. I came through the ranks.

Bet you didn't know there's a Scottish football team named after a soft, mild, creamy cheese, and ex-pundit Jimmy Hill's most distinctive feature? It Brie Chin City!

Our leading scorer, it's OG.

I saw a sign on the motorway, which said, Incident, slow down. When I got there, it was Paul Ince, stopped on the hard shoulder, with a big dent in the side of his door.

The angler's football team aren't having the best of seasons, perched just above the relegation zone. I can't understand why. I mean, no one can deny they know where the net is.

We've drawn the cough mixture amateurs in the 1st round of the cup. I keep telling the lads not to count their chickens: there are no wheezy games, nowadays.

Michu had soldiers in bearskins and red tunics, poking out of the top of his socks. I think they were his shin guards.

I hear we've just signed a descendant of Cochise. Brave decision if you ask me.

What would you get if you crossed a wading bird with the Potteries most famous football club? Stork City!

The pitch was so waterlogged the groundsman got into difficulty. It was looking really dicey...then the woodwork came to the rescue.

I've just seen a referee, trading in a set of goalposts. He post pawned them.

After months of trying, we finally managed a clean sheet: we boarded the goals up.

That new meat factory that's opened near us: I've heard a couple of footballers have got a steak in it.

I said to the manager of LA Galaxy, if you had $32,000 in one hand and $32,000 in the other, who would you buy? He said, that's the $64,000 question.

Wayne Rooney's new haircut: it's dire follicle.

I would have given my right arm to be an international goalkeeper...

The referee quizzed Northern Ireland's captain upon why the team had taken to the field with Afro-Caribbean trumpeters, percussionists and drummers, clinging to their sleeves. He said, try asking the boss: he was the one who said to wear black arm bands.

I buy my alcohol from the retired German footballer, who's opened a shop at the bottom of our street. If you're ever in the area, look out for it. It's called: Oliver's Beer-off.

David Beckham was boarding a flight in Tel Aviv. He said to the pilot, is your first name Pontius?

I went to the footy and there were all these half-man-half-horse type creatures, crowded together in the middle of the field. It was the centaur circle.

He said, do you fancy a few bob on the brickies' football team to get a result at Upton Park? I said, what are the hods?

A referee's card joined the army, but then ran a mile when it was posted to the front line. A statement from the military confirmed it was yellow.

Is Puss in Boots a feline footballer?

I could hardly believe it when the Lone Ranger's horse popped up to score the winner. Talk about a Silver goal.

What would you get if you crossed a pair of bifocals with a spud? A spec-tator!

Foggy was clean through on goal. He mist.

Norwich City drew the Illusionists XI in a third round tie at Carrow Road. When the match kicked off, I spotted this bloke, sawing a woman in half in the penalty area. Not that anyone was surprised: it was the magic of the FA Cup.

I can't believe Roman Abramovich has installed a tin of gelatinous pork shoulder as his new manager. It's Spam Allardyce.

That cub with the bow tie, the one who hangs around with Yogi Bear, he's taken up football. Not that he's any good. Last time I watched him play, he got Boo-Booed off the pitch.

We play with an orange ball when the snows come. Goodness knows why. Whenever it gets a good kick, it splits down the middle and leaks juice and pips.

Our full back crept up behind United's star winger and banged a gong, causing him to lose concentration and give up possession: it was a sly ding tackle.

I bet you didn't know Kyle Walker had two brothers, one called Hill and another called Cliff?

The boss reckons my best position is left back: left back in the blooming dressing room.

Hang on a minute, he must have had three brothers called Cliff...and it's just been on the news that they've all fallen off a mountainside!

I made my debut for Slimmer's World in the first round of the cup, but was disappointed as we went out with a whimper. We just weren't hungry enough.

Our centre half had a good game, mind. High crosses were like food and drink to him.

Caveman United: don't try and tell me it's a big club.

The boss substituted me after I gave twenty balls away in the first half hour. As I trotted despondently up the tunnel, he said, do you know those things cost seventy-five quid apiece?

I couldn't believe my eyes when this football commentator arrived to repair my roof. I thought, whey hey, it's Martin Tiler.

Trapattoni instructed the Irish football team to practise return passes, so they clubbed together and bought eleven two-way tickets from Dublin to Cork...

I went to watch Hastings United play. The official attendance was 1066.

Llanfairpwllgwyngyllgogerychwyrndrobwllllanty siliogogogoch FC versus Borussia Mönchengladbach...it's a hard one to call.

The former attic conversion specialist we've signed is a complete joke. He's got two loft feet for a start...

Short-sighted footballers: they don't see much of the ball.

I've just watched a football match in a corridor. It was a wonderful passage of play.

The kid we've got playing central defence, the one who used to work in the call centre, he's fantastic at holding the line.

Only worry now is his looming court case. He hated his job so much, the first thing he did when we offered him a contract was chop up all the communication equipment with a machete. He was arrested for phone hacking.

Did you hear about the Irish footballer who was convinced his clock had OCD? He said it wouldn't stop ticking.

I went to the game and stood on the kop. I don't think he was best pleased when he saw the state of his helmet.

Walcott gave the crowd a lift when he signed a new contract. He went home with sixty thousand supporters crammed into the back of his car.

Did you see that programme last night about the psychology of penalty shoot-outs? Unmissable.

What did the footballer say to the corner flag? Absolutely nothing. Why would he? A corner flag is a long stick with a piece of triangular cloth attached.

I went to watch Luton Town. I had a seat next to Lord Lucan.

The Barcelona boy scouts association football team: what's this I've heard about them getting a new camp?

Commentary: And it's a raking pass from Gardener...

I thought the autobiography of England's World Cup winning goalkeeper was excellent. That said, I never knew he became a famous street artist.

Referees: they know the score.

Vinnie Jones went to court, accused of assaulting a Satsuma. He got off on a peel.

Our chairman's just been on the radio, saying the manager's future is in jeopardy. Personally I've never heard of them. But I'd be interested in knowing if they've made an official approach...

We lost our first game in the underwater football league: we were playing too deep.

I'm in the second team at the jam factory. I'm in the preserves.

Apparently John Terry's lost his bank book. If anyone finds it, I've heard he heartily recommends the chapter on Barclays.

Lukasz Fabianski's visit to Islington's Polish Club didn't go down too well. It was filled with English people, drooling over tins of Kiwi cherry blossom and bottles of Car Plan T-cut.

I said, I've been asked to sign for a French football team. He said, Toulouse? I said, no, stupid, to win!

Benitez ushered Chelsea's first team squad into his kitchen and ordered them to climb on the big wooden thing in the middle of the room. He'd promised the chairman they would on top of the table by Easter.

What goes, broom, broom, broom, broom, broom? Arsenal's open top bus, reversing into the garage for another year...

A team from the Snakes & Ladders factory took on a team from the Ludo factory. It was a game of frequent counter attacks.

I went to this match, where every player on the pitch was called Neil. Guess what? It finished Neil-Neil.

Which team scores most of its goals in second half injury time? Late on Orient!

The new striker for one-armed bandit mechanic's XI: the manager reckons he's slotted straight in.

If you crossed an animated ghost with a Danish goalkeeper, would you get Casper Schmeichel?

The chairman gave the boss a transfer kitty and what does he do? Only goes out and signs Korky the Cat.

To be fur, it does have excellent purr-tential!

It was such a one-sided encounter that the keeper spent the entire match, swotting up on his algebra. As the final whistle blew, he closed the final page: it was a textbook finish.

I went shopping and came across this square, filled with wooden stalls, selling off professional footballers. I thought, ooh look, a transfer market.

The red Indians match against the gunslingers went to a shoot-out. Guess who won...?

Gareth Bale's had a big, red spot lanced: the Premier League have credited him with a cyst.

Where did James Bond stand at the big game? The spy on kop!

I was walking down our street and noticed a football match in the living room of number twenty-seven. It was obviously taking place behind closed doors.

The jockey's football team: they aren't half riding their luck...

HM Prison Strangeways' star striker has released a book about his life on the outside. Available from all good bookstores, it's called, How to Get Rich Quick by Robin Banks.

When we were promoted to the Premier League, I confidently predicted we would last three seasons. And we did: autumn, winter and spring.

I said, doctor, I can't stop thinking I'm Kenny Dalglish. He said, great Scot!

What's blue and smells like an Exeter City shirt? An Everton shirt.

I'm a massive Villa fan. I particularly like the big one, overlooking the bay in Palma Nova.

Stylianos Giannakopoulos: his name must be worth a fortune at Scrabble...

Footballer autobiographies: they're title rivals.

I visited Rory Delap's house and there was this revolting-looking blanket on the back of the sofa. It was a foul throw.

Norman Hunter was enjoying a tour of the Etihad when Roberto Mancini spotted him. Norman, he said, if the great Leeds United team of the seventies played Manchester City now, what do you think the score would be? Hunter said, probably a draw...mind you, we haven't trained for thirty years.

We all cried foul when our inside forward's upper arm exploded. The ref waved play on, ruling it was a shoulder charge.

I can't believe it: I've been offered a hundred quid a week to play semi-pro for Stretcher Bearers United. I'm just trying not to get carried away with it all...

This Barnsley fan attacked me. I escaped with miner injuries.

Dog fouling round our way is really getting out of hand. I was clean through on goal yesterday when I was tripped from behind by a rampaging Rottweiler.

When the former baker turned pro footballer signed a 100k per week contract with United, he proudly announced, I don't knead the dough anymore.

I was walking up this steep slope on my way to watch French side Newcastle United. My mate asked what I thought the score would be. I said, Toon hill.

Jupiter United supporters: what planet are they on?

I've just seen a bloke with a football match taking place on his back. I thought, whey hey, game on.

The boss threw himself in the river when we lost 4-0 on a pre-season tour of Egypt. I think he was in de-Nile.

Norwich City's new signing, the former Kwik Fit tyre fitter, according to the manager, he's all pumped up and ready to go.

I went to this match, where the crowd was filled with old ladies, exchanging prosthetic implants. It was Hip Switch Town.

The manager was wearing a long coat made from fresh fruit and laptop computers. It was his Apple Mac.

Did you hear about the hard up footballer who inherited a cat o' nine tails? He flogged it.

I spotted the assistant referee, scribbling notes on his inside thigh. I thought, ooh look, a loins-man.

Indiana Jones had a trial on the wing at Southend. He was a bit on the slow side, but couldn't half whip a cross in.

Two Villa fans were window-shopping outside Carphone Warehouse. One of them said, that's the one I'd get. Cyclops in a Blues scarf growled, you talking about me?

All seater stadiums: I don't know where I stand with them.

Q: What do you call an Arsenal fan opening a bottle of champagne? A: Waiter.

PLAYING IN THE HOLE

I arrived home just in time for MOTD, but missed it because the wife insisted upon watching a John Carpenter horror film instead. Next day, my mate rang and asked what I thought of Van Persie's second half hat-trick. I said, I don't know: I didn't see it because of The Fog...

The nudists' XI: they're on a right losing streak.

Here are tonight's beach football results: Bondi 2 Blackpool 1.

I've just been selected for the astronauts' football team. I can't believe it. In actual fact, I'm over the moon.

We've got a new defender called Rupert Ponsonby-Smythe. Honestly, he's different class...

Fulham's new centre forward is extremely comfortable on the ball. He's currently fast asleep in the penalty area, using it as a pillow.

Did you hear about the Irish footballer, who drove sixteen times across the Forth Road Bridge? He made a vociferous complaint to the Scottish Tourist Board, saying there was no sign of the other three.

I said, I can't believe it: Wycombe Wanderers have just won the FA Cup! Mum said, look, don't you think you've been on the Playstation long enough for one night...?

Footballer's lower legs: do they live in shin pads?

We're bigger than Man United. Their average height is only five-nine, we're all six-footers.

Commentary: And Warburtons centre forward is clean through. He only has the keeper to beat. He must score, must score....oh, no, he's sliced it wide!

I refused to go out on loan, so the boss sent me to Coventry...

My mate reckons Scottish side Dumbarton are named after a former Premier League footballer currently plying his trade in France...

The boxing ring company challenged the wrestling ring manufacturers to a game of football: it finished all square.

Who do I support? How does a wife and three kids sound?

This Burnley fan threw a pin at us. I said, run for your lives: he's got a hand grenade.

I've just had a call from this footballer, asking if I wanted to go halves with his inheritance. It was Jack Will Share.

Can you believe someone broke in the club storeroom and stole sixteen cases of Red Bull? Honestly, I don't know how they sleep at night.

In the wake of his latest failure, Fernando Torres was spotted eating bars of milk chocolate with a caramel and biscuit filling. I guess he needed a Boost.

That bald-headed referee's chief from Leeds: if you ask me, he's got the life of Riley.

I asked this bloke called Roy what he thought of his name. He said he wasn't Keane.

This ball growled at me. It was football mad.

If you see anyone attempting a scissor kick, stand clear...or you might find yourself with an unwanted haircut.

The shift supervisor from the wool factory, the department that manufactures garments for the lower leg and foot, he took over the running of the works' football team recently. After a dozen straight defeats, the crowd began to sing, socked in the morning, you're getting socked in the morning, socked in the morning...

I know nothing about football but everything about sweets. I'm Tic-Tac-ally astute.

Aston Villa's pooches challenged Southampton's pooches to a scrap after the match. It was a real relegation dog fight.

It's been announced that, with regret, the glue factory football club is now officially insolvent.

Torres blasted the ball over the bar. As it whizzed past my head, I heard it say, lend us a fiver. I thought, another chance goes begging.

I've just paid under a tenner for an eight yard strip of turf, painted white. It was a goal line clearance.

Football magazines: I've got a few issues...

Did you know Vinnie Jones still keeps clippings of his numerous on-field encounters? They're in his scrap book.

Watching Super Sunday on my new Panasonic 55" flat screen TV, I said to my mate, any idea who invented televisions? He said, some bloke called John Logie. I said, how do you know that? He said, a little Baird told me.

This sign outside the football ground said, CCTV in operation. I thought, cripes, I hope it's not serious.

I'm not saying I'm unlucky, but when I booked on a cruise, the last place I expected to dock was Port Vale.

The overweight football team: they're firmly entrenched in the bellygation zone.

We drew Leeds in the cup. We drew them climbing into the famous old trophy on a sheet of A4, using pencils and crayons.

Lionel Messi's house is really weird. Instead of a bell, he has lots of multi-coloured, helium-filled rubber things to pop: it's his balloon d'or...

I understand the gaffer openly admits it was a mistake, selecting our top scorer with a broken leg. I've never seen such a limp performance.

The referee said, play on...and the cast of A Midsummer Night's Dream appeared and began performing in the penalty area.

We played this really bad tempered team from Glasgow. I think their nickname was the Grrrs...

The big match between the cardiologists and the cartographers, it was superseded by a ticker tape welcome.

I'm gutted we've drawn Bayern in the next round. I'm beginning to fear the bratwurst.

David Bowie's sponsored football team is really struggling for form. Advisors have told him it's time he made Changes.

The tramps association have formed their own footy team. Good luck to them, I say. I mean, it's not as if they've anything to lose, is it?

I couldn't believe it when the Hammers went one down against the amateurs from the alarm clock factory: it was a real wake-up call.

We lost 3-0 in the end. When I told my dad, he said, you've got to be winding me up...

As soon as I got in the ground, I could hear this put-put-put-put-put noise. It was the misfiring striker.

The crowd went crazy when Wenger sent the Gunners out with a dog lead apiece. They were obviously going to try and walk the ball in again.

I trapped the ball. I dug a big hole, covered it with branches then sat and waited until it fell in.

The red Indians won 2-1 away at LA Galaxy: quite a scalp...

On a tour of the UK, the red Indians team coach broke down on the motorway. Police discovered them on the central reservation.

It was the monkeys who came out on top in the jungle world cup final: Chimpioni, Chimpioni...

Former Arsenal star Paul Merson went to the casino and spent £5000 on chips. They were still frying at four in the morning.

I'm an Eagles fan. My favourite song is Hotel California. Oh, and by the way, I think Crystal Palace are rubbish.

ET's been caught stealing from the club shop. I always said he was light fingered.

Did you see Steve McClaren on Mastermind last night, answering questions on Dutch professional football? He was a right old clever clogs.

I nipped out for a quick pint and there were two footballers, baring their backsides at the bar: it was Wayne Mooney and Rude Van Nistelrooy!

We've just signed a player called Col Lision: he's an impact player.

Apparently a bloke in a dinner suit turned up at Old Trafford yesterday and put a bid in for Robin Van Persie. It was a formal offer.

We played the Pinocchio appreciation society in a pre-season friendly and went one behind soon after kick off. We managed to get the better of them in the end, but I'll tell you what: they aren't half difficult to break down once they get their noses in front!

Chelsea will always be up there: it's the law of have riches.

I went to watch England play Brazil in Rio. I said, I wish I'd come in the car. My mate said, what, are you stupid? It's six-thousand miles down here. I said, I know, but I've left the match tickets in the glove-box.

David Beckham enjoyed his new Lord of the Rings DVD so much, he got straight on the phone to WH Smith to see when the book was out...

The midfielder we signed from County Cork has energy to burn. Remember the name: it's Luke O'Zade.

I went on this away day and the entire crowd were wearing hairpieces. Just in case you wondered, we were playing Wig On Athletic.

Did you hear about the Milwall fan that rang a personal injury specialist? He'd been banged up for three years for football related GBH and wondered if they had any jobs going!

I wrong footed the defence. I nipped in the opposition changing rooms and swapped all the boots round.

The attendance for England's 3-0 home defeat to Italy was almost a hundred thousand. An FA spokesman, puffing on a big, fat cigar, said he was disappointed with the result, but that the real winner was footfall...

Why was the full back claret and red? Because Messi had turned him inside out!

I've agreed to sign for the furniture polish works' football team: I've given them my Pledge.

Seventies footballer, Gerry Daly: was he was named after his parent's favourite German newspaper?

Speaking of which, David Beckham thought Tom Daley was a newspaper for alley cats.

After winning five games in a row to steer clear of the relegation zone, the manager of the lumberjack's football team warned, we aren't out of the woods just yet.

He was right. They went down in the end and he was axed.

I'm a big Forest fan. My favourites are Sherwood and Delamere.

Our centre forward slid the ball home then popped his clogs. It was a last gasp equaliser.

After another heavy defeat, Charlton's players stripped naked then departed post haste up the tunnel. In his post match interview, the manager said they left everything on the pitch.

There's this massive football competition taking place, contested by teams of walnuts, encased in milk chocolate and vanilla fondant: it's the Whirled Cup.

I attended a game in the local park, where the players ate mallets at half time instead of oranges. I thought, what a bunch of hammer chewers.

It's just been announced that, as part of a cost-cutting exercise, Hartlepool United's first team squad will now be salaried in raisins: wages will be paid directly into players' Currant accounts.

Did you hear about the angler who turned pro footballer? He was carped twenty-eight times for England.

The snakes beat the lizards at football: they did it in addered time.

I thought the vicar was doing a grand job, managing the choir boys' football team. After six defeats in a row, though, I can't deny I'm starting to lose faith...

When the gaffer announced he'd signed a new target man, the last thing I expected to see was someone with red, blue and white roundels painted on his forehead!

What did the manager of the margarine factory XI say to the team after defeat to arch rivals, Lurpak Rangers? We've got to do butter than that...

I arrived at the ground to discover the grass, shivering. I thought, ooh look, a frozen pitch.

The Irish footballer reported to the police station after being stopped for speeding. The sergeant said, you were going a bit fast, weren't you? What gear were you in? He said, same as I'm wearing now: my Nike T-shirt, trackie bottoms and trainers...

Is a cross bar where angry footballers go to drink?

Rooney ran on the field, munching a tuna and mayonnaise sandwich. It looked like Fergie had given him another free roll.

I've packed in playing for the botanists' footy team. I was sick of all the root one stuff.

What would you get if you crossed Arsenal's former assistant manager with Manchester United's French international full back? Pat Rice Evra!

It's been revealed that Reading are in talks to sign a free agent. Rumour is it's James Bond.

This Spanish goalkeeper appeared, wearing a backpack and feeling his way with a stick. I thought, ooh look, Hiker Cassilas.

All our new signing ever talks about in his post-match interviews are nails, pins and staples. As you may have gathered, he's very a-tack minded.

I'm a former Man United star. Order a picture of the club's Christmas nativity and you can just see me, twinkling in the corner.

Did you know that Elizabeth Taylor's husband once had a game of hide and seek in Staffordshire? They even named the local football team after the event: it's Burton I'll be on...

In an unprecedented move, Southend United have recruited a former British Rail employee as their new manager. Now, now, no need to scoff: word is he's got a brilliant track record.

That big log, playing out wide, shrouded in fog...it's a right wing ex-tree mist.

I gave a penalty away. I got this speeding fine and paid my mate a hundred quid to take the points for me.

The assistant referee said Giggs was fractionally offside: Sky Sports confirmed it was ¼ of an inch.

I hear AVB lost his job this morning. He nipped out for a sandwich then couldn't find his way back to the ground.

Our keeper was under so much pressure after a string of poor performances, he tried to commit suicide by jumping in front of a train: it went straight through his legs.

I got my cup final tickets on the black market. It was a Spivotal moment.

When I first heard that Mayan calendar lark, that the world was about to end, I thought, I'm going to stand next to Alex Ferguson: at least then I'll be guaranteed ten minutes added time.

Did you hear about the chiropodist, who was sent off for clipping an opponent's heel...?

Sportsflash: Scunthorpe United face a stiff test today after it was revealed the laundry lady mistakenly used starch concentrate on their kit.

I spotted 'the Special One', turning up a dead end street. I thought, no way Jose.

He said, what was Arsenal's last trophy success? I said, was it the egg cup?

There's still no sign of the new signing from Iceland: I reckon the boss has got cold feet.

I played against this winger on Saturday, who had a telephone in each shoe: he rung footed me all night.

We were lining up to defend a corner when this pub went flying over our heads. It was the Inn swinger.

INSIDE FORWARD

I scored with a thirty yard drive. What my parents will say when I tell them I'm going out with a big lump of ready-mix concrete is anyone's guess.

What would David Beckham be called if he became a referee? David Bookham!

This cannibal asked me why footballers spit so much. I said, perhaps you're leaving them on the barbecue too long.

If German third division players were English, what would they be? Superstars!

I understand Ronaldo has treated himself to a new golf club. Apparently it's Gleneagles!

There was this football match being played on thin ice, and the centre forward was having an absolute stinker. As he went clean through on goal once more, the crowd shouted, put your foot through it...

6-0 up after half an hour in our match against the park gardener's football team, we took our foot off the accelerator. We wanted to spare their bushes.

The manager of Olympique de Marseille had just settled down for the game when his phone rang. This voice said, can I speak to Joey Barton? He said, I'm afraid he's unavailable at the moment, the match has just kicked...hang on a sec', he's been sent off. I'll put him straight on.

I didn't know what to think when the Lone Ranger took over as manager. Credit where credit's due, though: a month into the job and he's put Silver-wear on the table already...albeit his horse's saddle.

Keep an eye out for the air stewards XI: they're off to a flying start...

What about the Manchester United player who ate all the pies? It was Full Jones.

We've just signed Basil Brush. Word is he's a real fox in the box.

I've just taken over as manager of the hunger strikers' football team. We've got great potential, but I must admit the overall squad looks a bit on the thin side.

There's this Arab Sheikh, who runs his own private league, played on the series of football pitches, installed within the sports wing of his home. The only thing he doesn't have is goal line technology: contentious decisions are passed on to the Dubai-house goals panel.

The footballers' Christmas nativity play had to be cancelled when the organisers couldn't find anyone to play the parts of the three wise men.

I was watching the DNA results on Jeremy Kyle: it was 2-1 to the mother.

As a trainee accountant, on secondment to Brentford FC, I was invited along to the monthly accounts meeting: it was held in the bored room.

Bolton Wanderers played a pre-season friendly on a difficult sand and gravel surface. They won 4-1...on aggregate.

Coleen Rooney entrede a spede tipyng centost adn wno wtih sxi hendrud wrods purr munite.

I can't believe it, we've actually gatecrashed the Top Four. OK, so the Top Four is a new nightclub in Wigan, but it doesn't matter: we still gatecrashed it, didn't we?

Referee Mark Halsey went to see A Midsummer Night's Dream and immediately stopped the play...

Vinnie Jones submitted a passport application form. He got it in a headlock and it tapped out.

I bumped into Theo Walcott in the Co-op, wearing a hat made out of fifty pound notes. I thought, ooh look, a salary cap.

Ex-England goalkeeper and self professed art lover, David James, was asked to comment upon the Mona Lisa. He said, well, she was no oil painting.

I paid a visit to the Liberty Stadium, but it's the last time, I can tell you. It was filled with ex-cons, out on parole.

Our Sunday league strike force is made up two footballing GP's. I've never seen such clinical finishing.

Former footballer turned racehorse trainer, Mick Channon, has been taken to hospital after taking a tumble, whilst out riding. A spokesman described his condition as stable.

Did you hear about the footballer who stole a calendar? He got twelve months.

I said to this waiter in the Anfield club restaurant, this meat's tough as old boots. He said, you're in Liverpool...what do you expect?

The ball was dipping under the bar...it was getting ready for a game of hide and seek with the corner flag, the referee's whistle and the goalposts. The referee's whistle was eventually on.

We've just signed Santa from Lapland United: we discovered a release Claus in his contract.

I put Football Focus on and Ryan Giggs was suited and booted with a string of trophies tied round his neck. I thought, ooh look, a cup tie.

The new under-soil heating at the KC Stadium is fantastic. No danger of postponements now. Hull will freeze over first.

Frank Lampard was relaxing on the beach when this car pulled up and all these gangsters got out and started Tommy-gunning the sea. It was a drive buoy shooting.

I saw four Rochdale supporters, having a game of football with a hedgehog. I was about to call the RSPCA, but then the hedgehog went 1-0 up...

Fergie's decision to play Dracula in goal wasn't his best. He was a brilliant shot-stopper but petrified of crosses.

In the post-match meal, he had black pudding...he wouldn't go anywhere near a steak.

When Dracula eventually retired, he moved into football management. The first thing he did was blood the youngsters.

I went to the footy and there was this player with a 100 watt bulb on his head. I think it was Lamps.

How do you know when a referee is contented? He whistles while he works.

I've just signed for the ornithologists' football team, but wish I hadn't bothered. I hate the fact we give the ball away so cheaply...

Who did the short-sighted ref bump into on his way to the opticians? Everyone he saw!

Commentary: And, with only two minutes left, the archaeologist's XI have taken a shock lead in this important fifth round cup tie here at Old Trafford. Travelling supporters are going absolutely historical...

I bumped into El Hadji Diouf, buying a CD. I said, what have you got, matey? He said, Bad Manners. I said, tell me about it: all you footballers are the same, spitting and swearing, every time you go on the pitch.

Fergie has just announced that he will be resting Wayne Rooney, Danny Welbeck and Howard Webb for next week's cup tie with Bristol Rovers.

I went to the game and there was this mobile disco, blasting out in the penalty area. Turned out it was DJ Campbell.

The attacker released by Accrington Stanley, he's now a tacker: he tacks floral covers to divans in the local bed factory.

What's blue and white and sits in a kitchen? A fridge with a Birmingham City shirt on.

2B's football team: they're a class act.

David Beckham arrived home, lathered in sweat, informing Posh that he'd lost the dog and had looked all over for it. She told him to look harder, so he shaved his head then went out and got himself a Chelsea Headhunters tattoo.

I said, don't you think it's about time they sent the sub on? He said, why? I said, the pitch is flooded.

Our first round match against the hen farm XI: it went down to the wire...

We played the council bin collectors in the next round: we were dumped out of the cup.

I got a job in Man United's laundry, but was in big trouble on my first shift when I got the whites mixed up with the coloureds and turned the kit pink. Honestly, they didn't half hang me out to dry...

Today's match stats: there are approximately 50 per box.

That bloke from Baywatch, I've just seen him disappearing off the field at the charity football match, with his buttocks snared between a pair of snapping, metal jaws. I thought, whey hey, he's been caught in the Hoff's hide trap.

I bumped into this Chelsea player, crying his eyes out. I said, Juan, what's the matter...?

William Hartnell was in goal, with a back four of Patrick Troughton, Jon Pertwee, Tom Baker and Peter Davison. In midfield were Colin Baker, Sylvester McCoy and Paul McGann, whilst Christopher Eccleston, David Tennant and Matt Smith made up the strike-force. I'm embarrassed to say they beat us 10-0. It was our own fault: we gave them too much time and space.

David Beckham has finally decided upon a retirement path: he's going on the after dimmer circuit.

It's just been raining footballers. Honestly, it was teaming down.

I've bought Four Season tickets. Not for the footy, silly: I'm off to see this vintage American pop group at Wembley Arena.

Did you hear about the defender who had six takeaways in one night? He was a full back.

I was sent on a scouting trip to give the once over on the constipation society football team, but came home unimpressed: there was complete lack of movement.

Aston Villa's first team squad are off to Rome on Sunday: roam round the back garden, wondering what went wrong this time...

It was 0-0 against the shoelace factory football team with only a minute to go. They thought they'd got away with a point: then a defence-splitting pass finally undid them...

Sunday league division one team, the dusty carpets...they've never been beaten.

I was watching the House of Commons football team and there was this Labour politician, who was brilliant in the air: it was Ed Balls.

Negotiations to sign the promising young market place attendant have now stalled.

I put MOTD on and there was this dog, commentating: it was Mutty...

It's just been on the Vidiprinter: the ducks' football team, they're a goal down...

The sponsor of the newly formed chicken league has been announced: it's Hen Power.

I'm writing a novel about Swindon Town, winning the Premier League. My mates think I've lost the plot, but don't know what they're talking about. It's in the cupboard under the stairs.

Why was there a Chubby Checker CD and a lathe on the edge of the area? Because Messi had been twisting, turning...

The Staffordshire Pottery Company: their name is on the cup.

I only get selected when it's been raining for weeks and the ground is saturated: I'm a mudfielder.

Two teams of washing powder had a game of footy: it was very much an Aerial encounter.

This referee walked into a hotel. He said, I'd like to book a room, please.

I was having a chat with seventies' footballer, Frank Worthington, but barely heard a word he said. His tie was too loud.

What do you call a Port Vale supporter at Wembley Stadium? Lost!

The artificial limb XI: we beat them over two legs.

I couldn't stop laughing when Steven Gerrard disappeared down a big crater, during the match at Upton Park. The crowd started singing, one joke hole, there's only one joke hole, one joke hole...

Arsenal's new shirt sponsors have reneged on what looked like a done deal at the last minute. A prominent pet food company, it was thought the team would look a bit silly with Winalot plastered across their chest.

I've got my goalkeeper cousin coming to stay with us over the weekend. Best make sure the sheets are clean.

We've just signed a player who's scared of sun, wind, rain, hail, sleet, snow, mist, fog, thunder and lightning. He lives in a climate of fear.

When Joey Barton mentioned me in his autobiography, I thought, crikey, I'm in the bad books now.

I asked this Scotsman to name his favourite football team. He said, Motherwell. I said, she's a bit arthritic during the winter months, but otherwise she's fine, thanks. Now then, who do you support...?

We lost 16-0 at the weekend. To be perfectly honest, we were lucky to get nil.

Commentary: And it's Evans to Murgatroyd. Oh, what a brilliant pass...

At the end of the match, all of the players dove into a big pool of water. It was a group puddle.

I can't believe Spurs' Welsh international wing back would risk his entire career by stealing a combine harvester. But it's true: he's currently out on Bale...

The local operatic society is thinking of putting a team out, it's just a case of finding the right pitch.

We're lying second in the league. We're not really. We're rock bottom. We're just lying about being second in the league.

I went to the footy and bought a programme. I can't believe it: I own football Focus!

Our misfiring striker actually hit the bar yesterday. He woke up next morning three sheets to the wind and two hundred quid lighter.

I reckon Johan Cruyff's son was born in Newcastle. I mean, why else would he call him Jordi?

Spanish footballers: are they made from liquorice?

I went to watch Everton play Liverpool and everyone in the crowd was drinking diet coke and tucking into healthy foods. It was the Local derby.

Northampton Town's manager came in my shop yesterday, ranting and raving: I shooed him the door.

We're a team of half-cars, half-canines, and we've just drawn Man City in the cup. We're the Honda dogs.

I'm on the same level as Ronaldo. Well, I was, once: we stayed in the same hotel and he was in the room opposite.

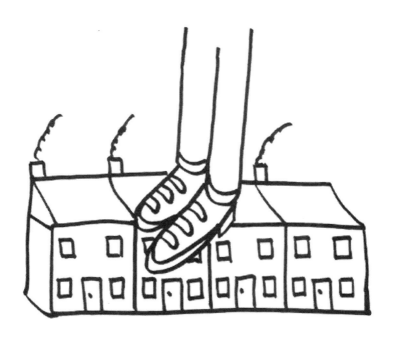

STANDING ON THE TERRACE